WALKING

IN THE

SUPER

NATURAL

WALKING
IN THE
SUPER
NATURAL

T. L.
LOWERY

WHITAKER
HOUSE

WALKING IN THE SUPERNATURAL

Dr. T. L. Lowery
Lowery Ministries International
P.O. Box 2550
Cleveland, Tennessee 37320-2550
www.tllowery.org

ISBN: 978-0-88368-659-1
Printed in the United States of America
© 2007 by Lowery Ministries International

Whitaker House
1030 Hunt Valley Circle
New Kensington, PA 15068
www.whitakerhouse.com

Library of Congress Cataloging-in-Publication Data
Lowery, T. L. (Thomas Lanier), 1929–
Walking in the supernatural / T. L. Lowery
    p.   cm.
Summary: "God desires every believer to manifest the supernatural as a normal part of the Christian life, preaching the gospel of the kingdom of God with accompanying signs and wonders as an end-time witness to all the nations of the world"—Provided by publisher.
    Includes bibliographical references.
    ISBN-978-0-88368-659-1 (trade pbk : alk. paper)
1. Supernatural (Theology). 2. Miracles. 3. Powers (Christian theology).
    4. Christian life. I. Title.
    BT745.L69 2007
231.7—dc22   2007001543

4 5 6 7 8 9 10 11 12 **W** 19 18 17 16 15 14 13 12

DEDICATION

This book is affectionately dedicated to

God the Father

whose great love sought us out when we were lost
and without hope;

God the Son

our blessed Lord Jesus Christ, who gave His life as
a ransom to redeem us and save us; and

God the Holy Spirit

whose anointing empowers and enables us to walk
and live in the supernatural and to minister with
effectiveness and power.

ACKNOWLEDGMENTS

When God laid it on my heart to share this special burden with God's people, I called together an impressive panel of special people whose wisdom and dedication to God I deeply respect. They are:

•*Pastor Stephen Lowery* •*Dr. Bill George*
•*Rev. Chip Pace* •*Mr. Dan Winters,*
•*Pastor Mitch Maloney* •*Dr. Steven Land*
•*Connie Broome*

They have been, and are, an invaluable spiritual resource and inspiration to the T. L. Lowery Global Ministries Foundation and to me personally. They gave suggestions and insights into how this vital message could best be shared in printed form.

I also wish to acknowledge my wife, Mildred, without whose love and assistance I could not have completed this book. She is not only the light of my life, but she is also a precious gift from God. Mildred, I love you.

—*Dr. T. L. Lowery*

CONTENTS

INTRODUCTION

Through the years, God has shown me that He is the same all-powerful God who revealed Himself to the children of Israel as Jehovah, the *supernatural* God who rolled back the Red Sea, rained down manna from heaven, caused water to gush from a rock, and miraculously delivered His people out of Egypt.

He has not changed! He has said, *"For I am the LORD, I do not change"* (Malachi 3:6). He is and always will be a supernatural God—a God of miracles, signs, and wonders.

Throughout the ages, He has continued to manifest His supernatural power. But as great and wonderful as the awesome miracles that God manifested on behalf of Israel were, and as great and wonderful as the remarkable miracles He manifested in the early church were, I believe the church of Jesus Christ hasn't seen anything yet.

The best is yet to come!

We are moving into a new and powerful time when God will reveal His glory as never before. Supernatural manifestations will take place not only in the form of healings and deliverances that have occurred in the past, but also in other demonstrations of God's power and glory we have not yet seen.

Within the body of Christ today, God's mighty power is already being manifested with creative miracles: there are reports of eyeballs forming in the sockets of people's eyes, cancers falling off, all types of sicknesses and diseases being healed, and people being raised from the dead. Miracles are happening today, but not on the scale of what is coming.

Before Christ returns—and I believe with all my heart He is coming soon—the church will move into a dimension and manifestation of His power and glory that is greater than any-thing we have ever seen or experienced. This demonstration of His power will bring in the harvest of the nations.

> **Before Christ returns, the church will move into a dimension and manifestation of God's power never seen before.**

The church, as a whole, is not currently operating in the unlimited, supernatural power God intends us to have. The average Christian is living far below what God has provided for him. While the majority of Christians believe God is a supernatural Being, and many even believe in His miracle-working power, they have failed to recognize Him as their own Source of supernatural provision. They have failed to come into a lifestyle where they believe and expect God to manifest Himself supernaturally on their behalf, through miracles, signs, and wonders, as He did for the children of Israel and the early church.

The apostle Paul said that he prayed this for the believers in the Ephesian church:

INTRODUCTION

The eyes of your understanding being enlightened...may [you] *know what is the hope of His calling, what are the riches of the glory of His inheritance in the saints, and what is the exceeding greatness of His power toward us who believe, according to the working of His mighty power.*

(Ephesians 1:18–19)

This is also my prayer for everyone who reads *Walking in the Supernatural*.

In writing to the Corinthian believers, Paul said, *"As it is written: 'Eye has not seen, nor ear heard, nor have entered into the heart of man the things which God has prepared for those who love Him'"* (1 Corinthians 2:9). When most people read this verse, they interpret it to mean it is impossible to know all that God has provided for His children. Yet Paul did not stop there! He continued by saying, *"But God has revealed them to us through His Spirit. For the Spirit searches all things, yes, the deep things of God"* (v. 10).

There is a powerful, invisible, supernatural realm that can be reached only through the power of the Spirit living and working within you!

It is my desire that the Spirit of the living God will hover over you and release fresh revelation to you so that you will see this spiritual dimension and, by faith, enter into it and begin to walk in the supernatural every day of your life.

Join me as we begin a spiritual journey with a goal to know God more fully as the almighty, supernatural God that He is, and to live our lives in the fullness of His supernatural power and glory.

CHAPTER ONE

SPIRITUAL MEGATHRUST

On December 26, 2004, a magnitude-nine earthquake shook planet earth. Pressure built up over nearly two centuries was released in a single snap. According to seismologists, the force of the quake, which was responsible for the stunning Asian tsunami, was the equivalent of .25 gigatons of TNT. The energy released was so huge that it caused the earth to wobble on its axis by up to an inch; it also changed the local geography, shifting islands by inches or feet and making a significant impact on the topography of the seabed.[1]

Geophysicists are calling it a *megathrust,* a term used for the most powerful of changes in the earth's surface.

A DYNAMIC MOVE OF GOD'S SPIRIT

I believe that what we saw happen in the natural realm has a parallel in the spiritual realm. A brand-new move of God's Spirit—a spiritual megathrust—is coming upon the church. It will radically change the lives of believers and move them into the fullness of what God intends for them on earth. The church of Jesus Christ will enter a new spiritual dimension whereby God will release His supernatural power in the greatest manifestation of signs, wonders, and miracles the earth has ever seen. This will occur in conjunction with the preaching of the gospel to the whole world before Christ returns—the one true light in the midst of widespread spiritual darkness, upheaval, and distress. (See Matthew 24:3–14.)

AN UNDENIABLE RECORD OF GOD'S SUPERNATURAL POWER

God's miraculous power is not limited to an "era of miracles," as some people suppose. He is the eternal, almighty God who has never changed. From the day God created the heavens and earth until today, awesome miracles, signs, and wonders have testified of His unlimited supernatural power. They have testified through such wonders as…

- the design and formation of the universe and humanity.
- the creation of God's chosen people out of the miracle child, Isaac.
- the deliverance of the Israelites from Egyptian bondage through miraculous signs and plagues.
- the miracles and healings manifested through the prophets Elijah and Elisha.
- the miracles and signs manifested through Jesus.
- the resurrection of Jesus from the dead after His sacrifice on the cross.
- the miracles manifested through the disciples and believers in the early church.
- the miracles worked through Spirit-led believers over the past two millennia.

SPIRITUAL MEGATHRUST

Yet as great as the awesome miracles, signs, and wonders were that He manifested through Moses on behalf of the children of Israel, in delivering them out of Egyptian bondage and during their forty years in the wilderness, such as...

- Parting the Red Sea
- Raining manna down from heaven and causing water to gush from a rock
- Revealing His power and glory on Mt. Sinai in fiery smoke and speaking to the Israelites with an audible voice
- Leading His people through the wilderness with a pillar of cloud by day and a pillar of fire by night
- Supernaturally providing for them and preventing their clothes and shoes from wearing out....

...as wonderful and mighty as the miracles manifested through the prophets Elijah and Elisha were, such as...

- Elijah shutting the heavens so there was no rain for three-and-a-half years
- Elijah calling fire from heaven to consume the sacrifice on the altar, proving Jehovah is the only true and living God
- Elijah raising a young boy from the dead
- Both Elijah and Elisha parting the Jordan River
- Elisha prophesying and a woman's barren womb being opened
- Elisha raising the woman's son from the dead
- Elisha involved in healing Naaman of leprosy
- Elisha causing an axe head to swim....

...and as powerful and awesome as the miracles manifested through our Lord Jesus Christ and the disciples in the early church were, such as...

- Jesus opening blind eyes, causing the deaf and mute to hear and speak, cleansing lepers, healing the lame, casting out demons, and raising the dead
- Jesus multiplying the five loaves and two fish to feed five thousand people, calming the raging winds and sea, and walking on water
- Peter healing and raising the dead, even his shadow bringing healing to the sick
- Peter's supernatural deliverance from prison by the angel of the Lord
- The other apostles manifesting signs and wonders, such as Philip performing mighty miracles and casting out demons
- Paul healing a man crippled from birth and raising a man from the dead....

...as great and wonderful as these miracles were, God does not limit Himself to specific manifestations or methods, and we must not limit His working only to the kinds of miracles He has demonstrated in the past. This includes the significant outpouring of His Spirit during the First Great Awakening in the 1800s, the awesome manifestation of His glory during the Azusa Street Revival that began in 1906 and impacted the world, the healing revival of the early 1950s, and even the widespread healings and deliverances we see today through the ministries of international evangelists. Within the next few years, I believe there will be such a

> **God doesn't limit Himself to specific manifestations or methods, and we shouldn't either.**

demonstration of signs, wonders, and miracles that there will be no comparison between the miracles God performed thousands of years ago and the miracles He will do in this end-time hour.

God still chooses to work miracles on behalf of those who reach out in faith to believe His promises. And He will do even more than He has before!

SUPERNATURAL POWER FOR THE LAST DAYS

In the twentieth century, we witnessed one of the greatest signs of Christ's soon coming—the rebirth of the nation of Israel and the regathering of multitudes of Jews to Israel from around the world after World War II. In fulfillment of prophecies and promises given to the Israelites thousands of years ago, God supernaturally manifested His power on Israel's behalf. The nation of Israel is a living testimony to the fact that God is still manifesting His miracle power. It is one of the greatest signs and wonders ever manifested to the world. The prophet Isaiah wrote,

> *Before she was in labor, she gave birth; before her pain came, she delivered a male child. Who has heard such a thing? Who has seen such things? Shall the earth be made to give birth in one day? Or **shall a nation be born at once**? For as soon as Zion was in labor, she gave birth to her children.* (Isaiah 66:7–8, emphasis added)

On May 14, 1948, in Tel Aviv, prime minister David Ben-Gurion proudly announced the establishment of the state of Israel. Between sunrise on one day and sunset on the next, Israel was officially recognized as a nation and was later accepted as a member of the United Nations.

Immediately after Israel was declared a nation, it was plunged into a war that threatened its survival; five Arab armies from Egypt, Jordan, Iraq, Syria, and Lebanon invaded it. Although the nation had basically nothing with which to fight, God miraculously intervened. When a cease-fire was effected eight months later, Israel had prevailed.

Almost two decades later, during the Six-Day War in June 1967, God once again supernaturally worked on Israel's behalf. Israel was surrounded on every side and greatly outnumbered in manpower, artillery, jets, and tanks. Egypt, Jordan, and Syria, with aid from other Arab countries, had joined together in an effort to completely annihilate the nation.

There was no way in the natural for Israel to win this war. Yet it was won because of God's supernatural intervention on its behalf. In just six days (eighty hours), Israel fought and won one of the most successful victories in military history, greatly increasing her possession of territories.

These awesome demonstrations of God's supernatural power, as well as many other prophetic signs that have been fulfilled, are like a loud trumpet blast heralding Christ's return. Just as God will continue to manifest His supernatural power in fulfilling His prophetic purposes for Israel in this end-time hour, He will manifest His power in bringing His church into the fullness of what He intends it to be, *"the measure of the stature of the fullness of Christ"* (Ephesians 4:13).

A POSITION OF POWER AND AUTHORITY

The *primary* sign Jesus said would signal His coming and the end of the age is found in the twenty-fourth chapter of Matthew. In answer to the disciples' question, *"What shall be the sign of thy coming, and of the end of the world?"* (v. 3 KJV), Jesus said, *"And this gospel of the kingdom will be preached in all the world as a witness to all the nations, and then the end will come"* (v. 14). The word *"sign"* in verse 3 is translated from the Greek word *semeion*, which refers to miraculous acts, visible demonstrations of God's power and authority. Manifestations of healing, deliverance, and other miracles will accompany and affirm the spoken word of the gospel as a witness to the world. God will pour out His Spirit in supernatural power to enable the church to fulfill the spiritual destiny of this end-time generation of evangelizing the world before Jesus comes.

> **Miracles will accompany the preaching of the gospel as an end-time witness.**

We must move *with* the coming wave of His spiritual power that will be a fulfillment of this sign, and not be overcome by it or left out of it. Christ has commissioned His followers to make disciples of all nations. Yet the church in its current state is not getting the job done. While we have made progress in fulfilling this divine directive, of the 6.5 billion people in the world, about 40 percent are considered unreached or least reached.[2] Our cities and nations are infested with demonic forces and satanic "strongholds." A stronghold is any place where Satan takes up residence and exalts himself above the will, plans, and purposes of God. Millions are bound by the powers of darkness and face the unspeakable horrors of war, poverty, death, and destruction. Thousands of people groups in remote areas have yet to be reached with the good news of Jesus Christ.

Something must happen to the church to bring it to the position of power Christ intended for it. God is going to prepare the church to fulfill His purposes and bring in a great harvest of souls before Jesus returns. As we draw near to Christ's return, therefore, an awesome demonstration of God's supernatural power will be released through the church to counteract Satan's stranglehold on the world.

A NEW SEASON

It is a new season for the body of Christ.

God wants us to set our eyes on the new things He will do in our midst. We will be equipped and prepared to walk in the supernatural!

Perhaps you think, "I'm not a pastor or evangelist. How can I be used by God to work miracles for His purposes?" Think of all the miracles God did in connection with the prophet Elijah. The Bible explains that Elijah was just a human being like the rest of us, yet God used him in miraculous ways. He will do the same with us.

The effective, fervent prayer of a righteous man avails much. Elijah was a man with a nature like ours, and he prayed earnestly that it would not rain; and it did not rain on the land for three years and six months. And he prayed again, and the heaven gave rain, and the earth produced its fruit. (James 5:16–18)

God desires to use "everyday" men and women—factory workers, business owners, doctors, teachers, carpenters, lawyers, and homemakers—right where they live and work, to manifest His mighty power to save and heal. He wants to breathe new life into the church to bring us to the place where He can use us in this way.

> *His intention was the perfecting and the full equipping of the saints (His consecrated people), [that they should do] the work of ministering toward building up Christ's body (the church), [that it might develop] until we all attain oneness in the faith and in the comprehension of the [full and accurate] knowledge of the Son of God, that [we might arrive] at really mature manhood (the completeness of personality which is nothing less than the standard height of Christ's own perfection), the measure of the stature of the fullness of the Christ and the completeness found in Him.*
>
> (Ephesians 4:12–13 AMP)

Christ gave the Holy Spirit to the church, and His plan is for us to grow and mature until we are living in a full manifestation of the Spirit and power of God. Our spiritual ignorance, fear, unbelief, and neglect have been quenching the Holy Spirit from manifesting Himself in our midst. Christ made every provision for us to have the supernatural gifts of the Holy Spirit flowing through us and enabling us to accomplish the work He has given us before He returns.

BEYOND KNOWLEDGE INTO EXPERIENCE

The twenty-first century church has reached a major turning point. We cannot and must not be guilty of denying God's supernatural, miracle-working power. We are facing crises and desperate world conditions unparalleled in history that can only be met as the church rises up in the fullness of the supernatural power of almighty God. Another generation is arising that desperately needs to see and experience His miracles.

My goal is not to cause you to focus on the miraculous, but to encourage you to fix your gaze on our supernatural God, who still works miracles on behalf of those who will dare to believe and trust Him.

As God's power and glory are manifested in the nations of the world through the church, doors for the gospel will be opened in countries now considered closed. Multiplied thousands will be saved, delivered, and healed. The Holy Spirit will reveal Jesus to all humanity in the fullness of His glory through the body of Christ. (See Ephesians 1:22–23.) The resurrection message of Jesus will be preached in a demonstration of the supernatural power of God with accompanying miracles, signs, and wonders as living proof that Jesus is who He claims to be, the Son of the living God.

> **God still works miracles on behalf of those who dare to believe Him.**

This end-time ministry will not be limited to church services or large evangelistic meetings, but will take place on the streets, in gang-infested areas and war zones in our cities, in drug dens, in the marketplace, in hospitals, in homes—anywhere people are hurting and enslaved to sin and Satan. As believers move into this powerful spiritual dimension, miracles, signs, and wonders will once again be an everyday function of the church in meeting the desperate needs in the world. Miracles will no longer be the exception but the norm!

SPIRITUAL MEGATHRUST

EXPERIENCING MIRACLES IN ALL AREAS OF YOUR LIFE

By reason of your spiritual birth, your heavenly Father deals with you in a supernatural way. He wants to bring you to the place where you are walking in the supernatural and experiencing miracles in every area of your life on a *consistent* basis. You therefore need to realize that every experience and circumstance in your life is another opportunity for God to supernaturally intervene, fulfill His promises, and work on your behalf. Walking in the supernatural does not mean there will be an absence of problems in your life. But when you have learned to keep your eyes off your circumstances and focus your spiritual vision on our miracle-working God, His power will be released into these situations—and healing, deliverance, and provision will be manifested.

LIVING TESTIMONIES TO GOD'S MIRACLE POWER IN THE WORLD

In my ministry, I have seen God's supernatural power manifested through tremendous miracles of healing and deliverance. One of the most outstanding miracles I will always remember was in the life of a man whose body was terribly crippled and twisted. His situation was totally hopeless—beyond any natural cure—until Jesus met him at his point of need, healed his body, and set him free.

I was in the Dominican Republic conducting an evangelistic crusade, and great crowds were coming to the meetings every night. People were getting saved and there were many miracles of healing.

One night, twenty thousand people were there, including many visitors and pastors from different parts of the United States. After I had preached and ministered for an extensive period of time, I was worn out and soaking wet with sweat. Just as I was ready to close the service and leave the platform, my interpreter asked me, "Brother Lowery, can you pray for one more person? We have a man who is crippled, and we want you to pray for him."

I didn't know how crippled he was. At that moment, some men were placing a man on the platform whose legs were drawn and twisted up under him. His arms were also twisted and drawn. Everyone in town knew who he was. He was the man whom people moved from one street corner to another so that he could beg.

I walked over to where he was lying. As I reached out to put my hands on him and pray, the Lord pulled my hands back. "I'm going to heal the man tonight, but don't lay your hands upon him. I must have all the honor and glory," the Lord told me.

I waited for a moment. By this time all the ministers from the United States and the missionaries had gathered around where I was standing.

Then I began to pray, *"Silver and gold have I none...."* Simultaneously, as I prayed, all the other ministers and missionaries began to pray the same thing with me:

Silver and gold have I none; but such as I have give I thee: In the name of Jesus Christ of Nazareth rise up and walk.

(Acts 3:6 KJV)

While we were praying, I heard the bones in the man's hands begin to crack and pop. He began to shake and tremble under the power of almighty God.

His hands straightened out!

By this time, it felt like my hair was standing up on my head and down the back of my neck.

He started crying and said, "It feels like there are some nails sticking in my legs." I believe this was the blood starting to circulate in his legs. He was shaking, and the bones in his legs were cracking and popping.

I took the man by his hand and lifted him up. This hopeless paralytic, who had been bound and twisted all his life, stood to his feet. He was as tall as I am. He started walking back and forth across the platform and pandemonium broke out.

> **The once-paralyzed man jumped off the platform and climbed over a cement wall.**

Upon seeing this awesome miracle manifested, seven to eight thousand people came rushing up to the front, crying and wanting to be saved. Throughout the years, when miracles have been manifested in my meetings, it has always resulted in a great response with hundreds or thousands responding to accept Christ.

The once-paralyzed man jumped off the platform and climbed over a cement wall about four feet high. I can see it now. He started walking down the road, and a man on crutches came out from the side of the road. The man on crutches placed his hand on the paralytic man who had been healed. He dropped his crutches—instantly healed by the power of God. He knew that if he just touched that man who had received such an incredible miracle, he would be healed. And he was!

Jesus promised us, *"He who believes in Me, the works that I do he will do also; and greater works than these he will do, because I go to My Father"* (John 14:12).

Throughout many of the nations of the world today, there are living testimonies to God's miracle power, such as the one I just described. According to reports I have read, there are widespread manifestations of tremendous miracles taking place in China and other nations, resulting in thousands of people coming to Christ. The following are just a few of the reports I have read in the last few years concerning miracles around the world.

CHINA

Paul Hattaway, founder and director of Asia Harvest, and his wife, Joy, reported the following:

In the West some Christians believe the day of miracles ended when the last Apostle died, or when the last book of the Bible was completed. In China the house church believers look upon such views as ridiculous and tragic. They see God perform miracles regularly, yet take no credit themselves, realizing it is all the work of God. They always acknowledge the greatest miracle of all to be a heart changed from darkness to light by Jesus' blood.[3]

SPIRITUAL MEGATHRUST

In the province of Henan, God's supernatural power is being manifested with miracles of healings, deliverances, and resurrections from the dead. The Hattaways reported,

> Miracles and powerful signs and wonders are a common occurrence among house churches in Henan. Healings, deliverances of demons, and other miracles often testify to non-Christians throughout the province of God's power and reality. We have even documented several clear testimonies of dead people being raised back to life. The Henan house church leaders are always careful not to focus on the miracles themselves, however, but prefer to focus on the Miracle Maker, Jesus Christ.[4]

Dennis Balcombe, pastor of Revival Christian Church in Hong Kong and founder of Revival Chinese Ministries International, shared the following testimony of a woman in China who was raised from the dead:

> An elderly Sichuan sister died of sickness and was buried. Three days later the Holy Spirit came upon a church member revealing that the sister had just returned from heaven and was alive. Accompanied by coworkers, the family members of the sister rushed to the graveyard. When the casket was opened, they saw the sister coming to life. For the next few years the sister never stopped testifying for the Lord until she was called home. The sister's return from [the] dead had tremendous impact on the gospel work locally. Many believed in the Lord and had stood firm in their faith despite severe persecution.[5]

INDIA

The Friday Fax, which provides news from India and around the world, gave these accounts from a doctor in India:

Surgeon Dr. Victor Choudhrie of Madhya Pradesh, India, reports that at the moment, it is mainly miracles that cause people to open their hearts for Jesus and, when they have heard more about him, commit their lives to him. "God is working predominantly through women and uneducated people," says Choudhrie. In July 2005 alone, Choudhrie knows of 352 people who have been baptised, 77 new churches planted, and 1,506 people who have been trained as church planters. The following is a selection of his recent reports:

The heavy rain in the monsoon period drives many snakes out of their territories and into the villages. That leads to many snake bites, and only lucky people can be treated in time. Mohit was in the forest with his herd when he was bitten by a snake. He managed to make it back to his village and tell people what had happened, then lost consciousness. Neither the snake charmers nor the village healer could do anything to help him. One of his neighbors asked a follower of Christ to pray for Mohit; 25 minutes later, he regained consciousness. Many people became open for the gospel through this miracle.

In Chattisgargh State, a deadly snake wrapped itself around a 15-year-old's hand during a church planting seminar. He managed to brush it off, but it fell on someone else. That person also managed to shake it off, and it finally landed on an open Bible. It died on the spot. The witnesses who did not yet know Jesus were astonished, and many have started following Jesus.[6]

MONGOLIA

Dennis Balcombe of Revival Chinese Ministries International also reported this incident of remarkable healing and the salvations that have occurred as a result:

> A 14-year-old girl accepted Christ in Inner Mongolia. "Anna" was eager to go out and preach the Gospel immediately! However, because of her youth, she was paired with a 20-year-old sister.
>
> Together, they travelled all over the countryside, preaching and witnessing to people. One day, they came upon a farmworker toiling in the fields. They began to preach to her but she deterred them, saying she had no time.
>
> "Go inside the farm house and talk to the old woman lying in bed," she muttered irritably. Anna was very excited! She had permission to preach!
>
> She entered the house and shared the Gospel with the elderly woman, who kept nodding her head like she understood, tears streaming down her face.
>
> Then the farm worker came rushing into the house, yelling at Anna, "She can't hear you, she's deaf!"
>
> But Anna retorted, "No, she does hear me. Jesus can heal and He has healed her!" The woman challenged

her, "If indeed Jesus can heal people, then have Him heal her of paralysis. She has not left her bed for years."

Excitedly, Anna exclaimed, "Yes! Yes! Of course He can heal her!" She ran over to the old woman and grasped her hands, gently urging her to stand on her feet. The old woman stood, and slowly began to walk!

Because of this miracle the whole family accepted Christ and today, they have a house church in their home![7]

This is just a small sampling of multiplied thousands of miracles taking place worldwide. These manifestations of God's miracle power will continue to increase!

FOUR MAJOR CHARACTERISTICS OF THIS NEW SUPERNATURAL DIMENSION

You may be thinking, *How will I know when this end-time move of God's supernatural power has begun?* There are four major characteristics of the coming new dimension and manifestation of God's power and glory that will position the church to bring in the greatest harvest of souls the world has ever seen.

1. God will bring about radical changes in the church to raise it to a new level of spiritual maturity and authority, so that He can use it as a channel through which He can pour out His miracle-working power.
2. God will bring the church to a new level of revelation knowledge whereby He will reveal Himself in intimate communion and fellowship. His glory will be manifested in the midst of His people.

3. There will be called-out believers who have given themselves fully to God and will be empowered to do the work of the ministry—not just well-known evangelists, pastors, teachers, and ministers.

4. Finally, as a wave of God's miracle power sweeps across cities, nations, and continents, the world will have a final end-time witness of the gospel of Jesus Christ preached in a demonstration of the supernatural power of God, resulting in an unprecedented worldwide harvest of souls.

WALKING IN THE SUPERNATURAL

Walking in the supernatural is a powerful spiritual *reality*—a level of living whereby God's unlimited power flows through our lives. It is a way of life Christ not only has made possible for the church, but also has planned for us to personally experience.

Again, this is not a "pie-in-the-sky" lifestyle where there is no pain or heartache and where everything we need is instantly provided. Yet in every trial and circumstance we face, we will be able to depend and rely upon God's supernatural power to intervene and make us victorious.

STEP INTO THE FLOW

Before I began writing this book, my son, Stephen, shared with me the following vision:

> In this vision God opened my eyes and showed me the river of God. As I looked more closely and observed the flow of the river, I noticed there were various levels of surge.

Near the bank of the river it was relatively calm. A little further into the river the current was a little stronger. But nearer the center of the river there was a powerful surge.

My eyes were drawn toward the banks of the river where I saw a group of people standing together. These people were discussing the water. They knew a lot about the water, its characteristics and the composition of the water. But they had not yet stepped into the river.

As I was pondering the meaning of this vision, God showed me there was a place for those who know the depths of the river of God, and who are in the middle of the flow of His power and glory, to assist those who have not yet entered to step into the flow.

This awesome move of God will be like a mighty, rushing river flowing throughout the nations. Like the great river of life the angel showed John issuing forth and flowing from God's throne (see Revelation 22:1–2), it will be a river of the Holy Spirit coming from the very throne of God, pouring forth and releasing new life, healing, and supernatural power and anointing. Everywhere it flows, we will see tremendous spiritual growth and many people coming into God's kingdom.

Have *you* stepped into the river of God?

Or are you like the people Stephen saw in the vision, who are still standing on the brink observing the river but not stepping in?

SPIRITUAL MEGATHRUST

Many Christians have heard about the river—God's glory and anointing. They know what the Word teaches about the manifestation of His miracle power flowing through His people. They may have seen or experienced the miraculous. Yet they have failed to take the next step of wading out into the deep—into the middle of the flow where they can be immersed in God's glory and power.

To walk in the supernatural and see the miraculous released in your life, you must be willing to get off the banks and move into the river of God.

> This awesome move of God will pour forth and release new life, healing, power, and anointing.

In Joshua 3:11–17, we read that as soon as the feet of the Israelite priests carrying the ark of the covenant dipped into the waters of the Jordan, the waters were parted, enabling the people to walk across on dry ground. If the priests had not taken those steps into the water, the people never would have been able to enter the Promised Land.

You may say, "What do I need to know and do in order to get into the depths of the river of God where I am immersed in His glory and power? How can I be used by God in this supernatural megathrust?"

Some of the things we will explore together include…

- what is hindering the miracle power of God from being manifested within the church.
- how Christ intends miracles to be a distinguishing mark upon every Spirit-filled believer.

- how miracles are to *accompany* you.
- how to raise your level of expectancy so that miracles are a normal occurrence in your life.
- keys to breaking through your natural environment into the supernatural.
- how to develop supernatural eyesight.
- how you are a supernatural being born by an incorruptible seed and possess God's DNA.
- how God intends for you to live in an atmosphere of His glory.
- how to have God's miracle power continually flowing through your life.

It is my prayer that, as you continue to read on, you will not just wade in the river, but rather jump in!

If you haven't yet ventured out into the flow of the river of God, don't hesitate one moment longer. Set your spiritual focus on the Source of the flow. Break through every hindrance and take the first step.

Perhaps you have waded out a little into the river but are comfortable and content to stay where the current is mild—where you have begun to sense His presence and power but have not yet experienced the fullness of His Spirit. Read on!

Let us go into the depths of the river of God where we can be submerged in His glory and power.

SPIRITUAL MEGATHRUST

PERSONAL APPLICATION

1. What is your personal experience in relation to miracles? Has God worked a miracle or miracles in your life? Write about it on a separate sheet or in a journal.

2. Have you witnessed a miracle in someone else's life? Describe the miracle(s) you have seen.

CHAPTER TWO

A NEW
PARADIGM

For the body of Christ to be ready for this new move of the Holy Spirit, we must experience some major paradigm shifts. A paradigm shift is a change from one way of thinking and doing things to another.

These shifts are driven by *agents of change*. The Holy Spirit is the ultimate Change Agent who effects God's purposes and plans for the earth. Yet God will use human change agents and earthly shifts in thinking and methodology to prepare the church and surrounding culture to receive a move of His Spirit.

For example, in the 1440s, Johannes Gutenberg's invention of the printing press was an agent of change that brought about a paradigm shift in the church and culture of that time. Before this invention, every book was copied by hand. This made books rare and expensive. With the breakthrough of the printing press, books not only became more readily available and easier to handle, but also were much less expensive to purchase. When the Bible began to be translated into languages the common people spoke, the mass production and distribution of the Bible to the people was a major key in bringing about the Protestant Reformation, as it gave people direct access to the Scriptures.

After a thousand years of medieval ignorance, knowledge of the Word of God exposed the decadence and corruption of the Church of that day. Protestant theologians, such as Martin Luther, led a reform movement placing strong emphasis on justification by faith rather than by works. There was also an emphasis on the right and responsibility of individuals to go directly to the Bible as their guide for living and having a relationship with God. A spiritual revolution occurred in the hearts and minds of people as they read the Bible and the Holy Spirit illuminated for them the Word of God.

A REVOLUTION IS NOT COMING—IT IS HERE!

What earthly agents of change do we see today? Two obvious and interconnected agents are the personal computer and the Internet, which have impacted individual, family, and business environments and are catalysts for a new paradigm shift.

> **Change your spiritual focus from only looking at the past to seeing what God is doing today.**

Over the years, we have been moving from a manufacturing, industrial society to a more organic, service-based, information-centered society. Connections between people with similar mind-sets, goals, and needs are being made around the world, not just locally or nationally. Communication that used to take days or weeks is now achieved in seconds. Change is inevitable. How we respond to this change may determine whether it is a positive or negative one for us. For example, while an information-centered society can bring isolation, it can also empower individuals to accomplish more, as well as open up new opportunities and methods for spreading the gospel.

You may feel content in your life and with the status quo in the church. You may not see the need for any changes. But the only way you will be able to embrace the new things God has for you in this hour is to let go of the old. Change your spiritual focus from only looking back at how God worked in the past to focusing on what He is saying and doing *today*.

MAJOR PARADIGM SHIFTS IN THE CHURCH

I want to highlight three paradigm shifts in the church that we are currently experiencing.

A SMALL-GROUP EMPHASIS

Perhaps as a response to a growing sense of isolation, combined with our service-oriented mind-set, a paradigm shift is taking place in thousands of churches around the world that are rapidly multiplying their numbers through the establishment of smaller "cell" groups of believers. These groups often meet during the week and supplement the larger, Sunday-morning gatherings; they are either part of or connected to a local church or denomination. Cell groups enable believers to have more personal interaction and fellowship with other Christians, and they provide more opportunities for teaching and ministering to people's basic needs.

A PARTICIPATOR MIND-SET RATHER THAN A SPECTATOR MIND-SET

Another paradigm shift, which will continue to intensify in coming years, is a change in thinking concerning the role of the believer within the local church. In many churches, believers sit back in the pews expecting the pastor to do all the work of the ministry. They listen to the sermon and may participate in the service by singing and lifting their hands during worship. Yet the vast majority of the congregation does not take up the role of ministry that Christ intended for them.

> Sadly, most Christians are not manifesting in their lives and ministries what Jesus said they could do.

The new paradigm shift does not limit healing, the working of miracles, and other important aspects of ministry to what is known as the "five-fold ministry" of apostles, prophets, evangelists, pastors, and teachers outlined in Ephesians 4:11. It seems as if, in the past, the church has stopped at verse eleven without paying enough attention to what follows it. Christ's purpose for His church has not changed. His plan is for every believer to minister to the church and the world. When He ascended to heaven, He placed the five-fold ministry in the church for the distinct purpose of equipping and building up believers so *they* can do the work of the ministry. *"His intention was the perfecting and the full equipping of the saints (His consecrated people), [that they should do] the work of ministering toward building up Christ's body (the church)"* (Ephesians 4:12 AMP).

Believers in the early church preached the gospel with boldness and operated in the supernatural gifts of miracles, healing, and deliverance. Nearly two thousand years later, it is sad, but true, to say that most Christians are not manifesting in their lives and ministries what Jesus said they could do.

Yet a fresh wind of the Spirit is blowing, and believers are beginning to rise up in power and authority to do the works of God that Christ has ordained for them, such as bringing people into the kingdom of God, healing the sick, delivering the oppressed, and even raising the dead.

This great truth—that Christ intends every believer to minister in His love and power—is not new to the body of Christ. In fact, for years, key Christian pastors and leaders have been teaching about "the ministry of the saints" in an attempt to get Christians out of their pews and into their communities, the inner cities, the marketplace—to begin to minister to people in every sphere of their lives and in every environment. However, although many Christians may have heard and clearly understood their role and ministry as believers, a great majority have failed to put them into practice in their lives.

While the reasons for this neglect may vary, *now* is the time for the church to rise up and for every true believer to take his or her position as a minister, stepping out in faith to do the works of God in a demonstration of His supernatural power!

Dr. Bill Hamon, author of the cutting-edge, revelatory book, *The Day of the Saints,* writes,

Very shortly, the Saints of God will begin demonstrating the supernatural works of Jesus on a scale that is unprecedented. Millions of born-again, Spirit-filled believers who have been trained and equipped will prophetically speak the words of Jesus and apostolically demonstrate His miraculous power as witnesses of the kingdom of God....

A "Day of the Saints" is coming in which God is calling every believer to participate. This will be the greatest time in history for those who hunger to fulfill God's will for their lives, especially those who are 100 percent committed to glorify Christ, overcome all things, reap the great harvest, and see God's kingdom come and His will be done on earth as it is in heaven.[8]

...We are going to see a mighty spiritual army of professionals, laborers, students, homemakers, and retirees demonstrating Christ Jesus' ministry and overcoming power over all the forces of darkness."[9]

While God will continue to use the important five-fold ministry to lead the church, it will no longer be just the evangelists and Christian leaders with well-known ministries doing the work of the ministry and being used in manifesting the supernatural power of God. It will be an army of believers who have received a fresh impartation of the Spirit and who are fully committed to doing the will of God and fulfilling the calling upon their lives. As members of the body of Christ hear the call of the Spirit, they will stop being *spectator* Christians and become *participators*.

I have observed this shift from spectator to participator in my crusades and other meetings. God's power and glory are being manifested in a dimension we have never before experienced. Our services are filled with a radical new breed of spiritual revolutionaries who are being transformed and empowered by the Holy Spirit to heal the sick and cast out demons. The word *radical* is defined by *Merriam-Webster's 11th Collegiate Dictionary* as "marked by a considerable departure from the usual or traditional." The Holy Spirit is breathing once again upon the dry, dead bones of the church and is bringing forth a spiritual revolution.

> **We need to stop being *spectator* Christians and become *participators.***

BEING THE CHURCH INSTEAD OF JUST GOING TO CHURCH

Along with this increase in participation, a paradigm shift and corresponding spiritual revolution is taking place among Christian young people who are tired of the status quo and are hungry for the reality and manifestation of the true power of God.

George Barna is a respected pollster and analyst of the American church and culture. In his recent book *Revolution,* he discusses what he calls a major shift now taking place that he believes will radically change the structure of the church as we know it. According to years' worth of data collected by Barna, the church is undergoing the biggest revolution of our time. Here are some excerpts from his book:

A quiet revolution is rocking the nation. The media are oblivious to it. Scholars are clueless about it....And Christian churches are only vaguely aware that something seems different, but they have little idea what it's all about.

Let me be the first to welcome you to the Revolutionary Age.[10]

...[There is] a growing sub-nation of people, already well over 20 million strong, who are what we call Revolutionaries....

They have no use for churches that play religious games, whether those games are worship services that drone on without the presence of God or ministry programs that bear no spiritual fruit. Revolutionaries eschew ministries that compromise or soft sell our sinful nature to expand organizational turf.[11]

Revolutionaries zealously pursue an intimate relationship with God, which Jesus Christ promised we could have through Him.[12]

...These Christian zealots are radically reshaping both American society and the Christian Church. Their legacy is likely to be a spiritual reformation of unprecedented proportions in the United States, and perhaps the world.[13]

The Revolution is not about eliminating, dismissing, or disparaging the local church....[It] involves the remnant of believers who are obsessed with practicing the same...passions that defined the early church, in order to be agents of transformation in this world.[14]

A NEW PARADIGM

In this eye-opening book, Barna reveals the current status of churched, born-again Christians and concludes that the majority of local churches are not doing the job of making true disciples and meeting the spiritual needs of the people. According to Barna's research regarding Christians in America,

- …the typical believer…spends less time reading the Bible in a year than watching television, listening to music, reading other books and publications.
- The typical churched believer will die without leading a single person to a lifesaving knowledge of and relationship with Jesus Christ.
- Eight out of every ten believers do not feel they have entered into the presence of God, or experienced a connection with Him, during the worship service.[15]

While Barna's book has stirred some controversy within the church, we cannot overlook the fact that there are a growing number of Christians (he has identified at least twenty million as Revolutionaries) who are craving more than just the tradition and religious forms that are so prevalent within many churches today.

There is a hunger within the body of Christ that is deeper than ever before. I believe the Holy Spirit has placed a dissatisfaction—a holy desperation—within many Christians. They are no longer content to just go through the motions. They long for an intimate relationship with the Father that will result in their lives being transformed so they can effectively impact their world.

We know how to *do* church. We may even have wonderful church services, seminars, and conferences where we sense

God's Spirit moving. The musicians and worship teams may be moving in the anointing, bringing us to a deeper awareness of God's presence. Pastors may be preaching with great fire and conviction. Yet we still do not have the full manifestation of God's power, with miracles, signs, and wonders being released in our midst.

In these last days before Jesus returns, God is bringing forth men and women who love God above everything else and are desperate to see His power and glory revealed in their lives to help the hurting and the lost. It is an unquenchable desire to see and experience God's presence and a manifestation of His miracle power. I see this hunger as I go from city to city, and it is not confined to Pentecostal churches but is also evident within Baptist, Methodist, Lutheran, and other mainline churches, as well as within many independent churches.

> God is raising up those who long to see His power revealed to help the hurting and lost.

Something is stirring in the hearts of God's sons and daughters. They know they need more than what they are currently experiencing in their personal and corporate spiritual life. They have caught a glimpse of their heavenly Father and what He intends them to be. Their cry ascends to the throne of God, "O Lord, we long for You. We are hungry to know You in all Your fullness. Bring us into the Holy of Holies. Remove the scales from our eyes and allow us to see You as You are—the unlimited, all-powerful, everlasting King of Kings and Lord of Lords! Pour out Your Spirit. Release Your power and glory.

Take us into a new dimension of Your Spirit where Your miracle power is flowing unhindered through us to fulfill Your will in this hour. We have heard of the mighty miracles you worked through Moses, Elijah, Elisha, Peter, Paul, and others in the early church. Lord, do it again. Release Your miracle power and manifest Your glory!"

Is this the cry of your heart?

Are you ready for God to pour out His Spirit upon you, to change you and take you beyond your natural limitations? Are you ready to enter a realm of the Spirit that you have only dreamed about but have never realized was possible?

ARE YOU A SPECTATOR OR A PARTICIPATOR?

In this new season that God is bringing us into, all of us in the body of Christ—both leaders and church members—must be willing to humble ourselves, recognize our need, and cry out to God to transform us into vessels who are ready to manifest His supernatural power. We should do this until we press through every barrier that is hindering us from seeing His miracle power flowing in our lives and ministries.

This is not a time for believers to sit back on the sidelines. It is time for every believer to become a participator and, by faith, to move into this new spiritual dimension.

For a moment, I want you to focus on your current position in the body of Christ. Ask yourself…

- Am I a spectator or a participator?
- Am I comfortable with just being a good church member? Am I content going from service to service, listening to the

sermons, perhaps singing in the church choir, and participating in other church-related activities, but never venturing out of my "comfort zone" to share my faith with others, pray for the sick, and lead others to Christ?

Or...

- Is a deep spiritual hunger growing within me to enter this new dimension where God's miracle power is flowing through me?
- Am I willing to let go of the old and allow God to change and transform me?

If you are willing, then let's prepare to walk in the supernatural!

PERSONAL APPLICATION

1. The Holy Spirit is breathing once again upon the dry, dead bones of the church and is bringing forth a spiritual revolution. Are you one of the revolutionaries God is raising up? Respond to the following questions:

   - Am I tired of churches that play religious games, worship services without the presence of God, and ministry programs that bear no spiritual fruit?
   - Am I bothered by the compromise that is in the church?
   - Am I dissatisfied and discontent to go with the flow?
   - Am I passionately pursuing an intimate relationship with God and willing to do whatever it takes to make Him the center of my life?

2. This is a new season for the body of Christ. If you have not already done so, move from being a "spectator" Christian to being a "participator." Ask the Father to show you opportunities in your community and city to minister to the desperate needs that are there. Look for every possible opportunity to share your faith, lead others to Christ, and pray for the sick. As you minister, believe that God will release His miracle power through you as He did through the believers in the early church.

CHAPTER THREE

ARE YOU
READY TO WALK
IN THE SUPERNATURAL?

O ne of the greatest dangers the church of Jesus Christ faces today is not an outside force, but something that originates from *within*. It is not the hordes of demonic powers or ungodly antichrists and anti-Christian forces working to tear down and destroy Christian values and everything that is pure and holy. It is not the threats of extinction or persecution by atheistic, godless rulers, dictators, or the religious systems of our day. With all my heart, I believe one of our greatest dangers is that of forgetting or denying our rich spiritual heritage and the supernatural, miracle-working power of almighty God that gave birth to the church.

Many of us love to talk about God's power that was released through the apostles and other believers, but we skip over the things we don't understand or that make us uncomfortable, and therefore we do not pursue God and His ways as we should. For instance, we focus on following the example of Acts 2:42, *"And they continued steadfastly in the apostles' doctrine* and fellowship, in the breaking of bread, and in prayers." When it comes to applying verse 43 to our lives, however, *"Then fear came upon every soul, and many wonders and signs were done through the apostles,"* we hesitate. We mumble through verses like Acts 5:12, *"And through the hands of the apostles many signs and wonders were done among the people,"* and Acts 6:8, *"And Stephen, full of faith and power, did great wonders and signs among the people."* The reason *why* we mumble through these verses is that we are not seeing the same thing in our own churches.

We make excuses for the absence of the miraculous. Some Christians are afraid to acknowledge the fact that these things indeed happened, because then they would have to answer the question of why they are not seeing miracles themselves. Others affirm that God worked miracles for the children of Israel and manifested His miracle power in the early church. However, they cannot believe that He would work a miracle on their behalf. Even more foreign to them is the thought that God would work miracles *through* them.

> **Some people find it hard to believe that God will work miracles *for* them and *through* them.**

These attitudes and perspectives are weighing us down and preventing us from stepping into the new things of God. To walk in the supernatural, therefore, our minds must be transformed by the thoughts and ways of God. (See Isaiah 55:8.) The apostle Paul admonished us, *"Be transformed by the renewing of your mind"* (Romans 12:2). Empty religious traditions, man-made doctrines, and methods of worship that are void of God's anointing must go. The new things of God will not fit into our old mind-sets, where we limit God according to how, when, what, and where we think He should work. We must get rid of every preconceived idea, as well as all doubt and unbelief, concerning the supernatural power of God, and allow the Holy Spirit to renew our minds to the truth revealed in God's Word.

WE SERVE AN UNLIMITED, SUPERNATURAL GOD

Those who say God no longer works miracles today are essentially saying He has ceased from being who He is. We serve a mighty, miracle-working God who has not changed, nor will He ever change.

Everything about Him is *supernatural*.

Everything He does is *supernatural*.

His book, the Bible, is a *supernatural* book. It was not written by a natural process; it was breathed into existence by God Himself. *"For prophecy never came by the will of man, but holy men of God spoke as they were moved by the Holy Spirit"* (2 Peter 1:21). The words contained in the Bible are not the compilation of human thoughts penned by human authors. God Almighty supernaturally inspired men who were submitted to Him, and they spoke and wrote under the power and direction of the Holy Spirit. Paul wrote, *"All scripture is given by inspiration of God"* (2 Timothy 3:16).

The writer of the book of Hebrews taught, *"For the word of God is living and powerful"* (Hebrews 4:12). God's Word is *alive!* It is not just a *source* of spiritual power—it *is* power. Paul declared that the gospel is *"the power of God to salvation for everyone who believes, for the Jew first and also for the Greek"* (Romans 1:16). The Bible is not a dry, dead book to be left sitting on a shelf gathering dust. It is a supernatural life source from our supernatural God. The writer of Hebrews went on to describe the power of God contained in His Word: *"Sharper than any two-edged sword, piercing even to the division of soul and spirit, and of joints and marrow,...[it] is a discerner of the thoughts and intents of the heart"* (Hebrews 4:12).

> **True sons and daughters of God are led, controlled, and directed by the Spirit living within.**

The Word of God is pregnant with the very life of God. Jesus said, *"The words that I speak to you are spirit, and they are life"* (John 6:63). The universe and everything in it is being propelled and maintained by God's Word. Jesus *"is the perfect imprint and very image of [God's] nature, upholding and maintaining and guiding and propelling the universe by His mighty word of power"* (Hebrews 1:3 AMP).

WE LIVE A SUPERNATURAL LIFE

Moreover, as born-again children of the Most High God, we are not born of a natural origin but a supernatural one. We are born by an incorruptible seed. *"You have been regenerated (born again), not from a mortal origin (seed, sperm) but from one that is immortal by the ever living and lasting Word of God"* (1 Peter 1:23 AMP). We must therefore not consider ourselves as mere physical beings who possess spirits, but rather live our lives on earth as eternal spiritual beings housed in physical bodies.

When an individual is born again by the Holy Spirit, his human spirit—once dead because of sin—comes alive again. He receives the Holy Spirit and the supernatural life of God within him. One of the distinguishing characteristics that clearly identifies those who are born again sons and daughters of God is that they are living their lives *in the Spirit*. The apostle Paul said,

> *The Spirit himself testifies with our spirit that we are God's children.* (Romans 8:16 NIV)

> *But you are not in the flesh but in the Spirit, if indeed the Spirit of God dwells in you. Now if anyone does not have the Spirit of Christ, he is not His....For as many as are led by the Spirit of God, these are sons of God.* (Romans 8:9, 14)

> *And because you are sons, God has sent forth the Spirit of His Son into your hearts, crying out, "Abba, Father!"* (Galatians 4:6)

The Word is clear: true sons and daughters of God are led, controlled, and directed by the Holy Spirit living within them. Life in the Spirit is a *supernatural* life. Aren't you glad you are a supernatural being, born again by the Spirit of the living God, and that His purpose for your life is that you walk in the supernatural?

THE CHURCH OF JESUS CHRIST IS A SUPERNATURAL ORGANISM

Not only are we individually God's children, but we are also part of a *supernatural* "organism" called the church. The church of Jesus Christ is not of natural origin, just as individual believers are not born again through natural means. When you were born again by the Holy Spirit, God Himself placed you within this *supernatural* organism. *"But now God has set the members, each one of them, in the body just as He pleased"* (1 Corinthians 12:18).

The very existence of the church is a witness to God's miracle power. God gave birth to the church through a supernatural impartation of His very life. He poured out His Spirit upon the followers of Jesus who had gathered together in response to Christ's command to wait for the promise of the Father. Jesus had given this charge to five hundred of His disciples just before He ascended to heaven:

> *Behold, I send the Promise of My Father upon you; but tarry in the city of Jerusalem until you are endued with power from on high.* (Luke 24:49)

> *Wait for the promise of the Father, which...ye have heard of me. For John truly baptized with water; but ye shall be baptized with the Holy Ghost not many days hence....But ye shall receive power, after that the Holy Ghost is come upon you: and ye shall be witnesses unto me both in Jerusalem, and in all Judaea, and in Samaria and unto the uttermost part of the earth.* (Acts 1:4–5, 8 KJV)

In obedience to this final charge, one hundred twenty of those five hundred—a remnant—were waiting together in Jerusalem to be baptized with the Holy Spirit. Ten days after receiving the charge, as they were united in prayer and waiting expectantly for this promise to be fulfilled in their lives, there was an awesome supernatural manifestation of God's power and presence that forever changed the course of their lives—and of the world.

The Holy Spirit was poured out on these believers on the day of Pentecost, and the church was born!

On Mt. Sinai, when God entered into a covenant with the Israelites, He manifested Himself in fire, smoke, the sound of a trumpet blast, and an audible voice. At Pentecost, He manifested His presence with a mighty, rushing wind and tongues of fire, and He spoke through the one hundred twenty believers in more than sixteen languages, declaring His mighty works. (See Acts 2.)

Christ promised His followers they would receive the power of the Holy Spirit to be His witnesses—to provide living proof that He is the Son of God and to testify to the truth of the gospel. He never intended for His church to be limited by its natural capabilities; He placed within it the supernatural, miracle power of God.

> **God never intended for His church to be limited by its natural capabilities.**

God's children receive supernatural gifts of the Holy Spirit, such as the word of wisdom, the word of knowledge, faith, gifts of healing, working of miracles, prophecy, discerning of spirits, the ability to speak in different tongues, and the interpretation of tongues. (See 1 Corinthians 12:7–11.) These various gifts are distributed for the benefit of the entire body of Christ.

All these [gifts] *are the work of one and the same Spirit, and he gives them to each one, just as he determines. The body is a unit, though it is made up of many parts; and though all its parts are many, they form one body. So it is with Christ. For we were all baptized by one Spirit into one body...and we were all given the one Spirit to drink. Now the body is not made up of one part but of many.*

(1 Corinthians 12:11–14 NIV)

God desired to have a people—His true sons and daughters—who together would bear His image and nature, and who would promote His purpose and vision while being fully conformed to His will. Your spiritual destiny and mine, as children of the Most High God, is to walk in the supernatural and fulfill His purpose upon the earth. His purpose in this hour is for His church to rise up and manifest Christ's glory and power to the world as a final end-time witness.

Throughout the Word, we read again and again of the miracle power of God manifested through the church. After the Holy Spirit was poured out at Pentecost, multitudes were saved and added to the number of believers. (See Acts 2:41; 5:14.) We read that *"through the hands of the apostles many signs and wonders were done among the people"* (Acts 5:12). The miracle power of God flowed to such an extent that people brought the sick and laid them on beds in the streets. Peter walked in the power of the Spirit to the point where, as he passed the people and his shadow fell upon them, they were healed. (See verses 14–15.) There was such a flow of the miraculous that a multitude came from the cities surrounding Jerusalem bringing the sick and demon possessed, *"and they were all healed"* (Acts 5:16).

Peter walked in the supernatural, and he healed the sick, cast out demons, raised the dead, and was supernaturally delivered out of prison by an angel. (See Acts 3:1–8; 8:36–41; 12:1–17.)

Paul walked in the supernatural, and God worked special miracles through him. Handkerchiefs were taken from his body and placed on the sick, and they were healed and their demons were cast out. (See Acts 19:11–12.) Paul healed a man crippled from birth (see Acts 14:8–10), raised a man from the dead (see Acts 20:9–10), and was supernaturally *delivered out of the mouth of the lion*" (see 2 Timothy 4:17) and from prison. (See Acts 16:16–40.)

Stephen, one of the seven laymen appointed by the apostles to handle the administration of the church's ministry to widows, walked in the supernatural. *"And Stephen, full of faith and power, did great wonders and signs among the people"* (Acts 6:8).

Another of the seven, Philip, was so greatly used in preaching the gospel and working miracles that people believed and were baptized. *"And the multitudes with one accord heeded the things spoken by Philip, hearing and seeing the miracles which he did"* (Acts 8:6).

The record is clear: The church was born through a mighty demonstration of God's power and *continued* to manifest the miraculous, which was an overflow of the power of the Holy Spirit in the lives of the disciples and other believers.

The true church of Jesus Christ is not a building. You did not become a member of the church simply by joining a local church assembly. The church is not merely a gathering of people on Sundays, Wednesdays, or other days of the week. You are not just a member of the Church of God, Assemblies of God, Baptist, Lutheran, Episcopal, or some other denominational or independent church. The church is not an organization controlled or governed by man. The church of Jesus Christ is empowered and directed by the Holy Spirit, and Jesus said, *"The gates of hell shall not prevail against it"* (Matthew 16:18 KJV).

From every country, tribe, and tongue—and from every walk of life—God is calling, separating, and consecrating a holy people and placing them in the body of Christ. The Holy Spirit is working in every nation on this earth—revealing Jesus, drawing people to Him, saving, healing, and delivering men and women out of the chains of bondage to Satan. Even in the midst of the hypocrisy, church politics, and spiritual apathy prevalent in the church today, God is preparing a people who will walk in His Spirit. Supernaturally, by the power of the Holy Spirit, the true church of Jesus Christ is being built as *"living stones"* (1 Peter 2:5)—members of the body who are vitally connected to Christ. Christ is joining them together and will bring them into full maturity in these last days, so that they are living and manifesting the fullness of His power.

> **You are part of an indestructible, supernatural superstructure, and the gates of hell shall not prevail against you!**

Two thousand years have passed since Pentecost, and the church still marches on. It has gone through periods of compromise, indifference, reform, and spiritual renewal. It has been continually under attack from Satan, who has attempted to dilute its message, detour believers from their task, and stunt its growth through fear and ignorance of God's Word. Yet God has preserved it and raised up a remnant for this end-time hour. You are part of a powerful, indestructible, super-natural superstructure, and the gates of hell shall not prevail against you!

OVERCOMING A SPIRIT OF RELIGION

We must learn to recognize and overcome hindrances to this spiritual calling. Again, the great danger we face in the church today, which would deter our purpose, is forgetting or denying the supernatural—overlooking the value and impor-tance of the miraculous and trying to rely on human ability and natural wisdom.

Many Christians are bound by a spirit of "religion" that is preventing them from letting go of their man-made doctrines and traditions. These are holding them back from experienc-ing this new move of God.

Jesus called many of the Pharisees and religious leaders of His day hypocrites because they were essentially *"making the word of God of no effect"* through their traditions, which they had handed down from generation to generation. (See Mark 7:6–13.) The same thing is happening in the twenty-first century church. People are holding on to man-made doctrines that have been passed down through the generations. They cannot receive the truth because human traditions have blinded them to it.

Despite reports from around the world about healings and miracles, a vast majority of pastors and denominations still teach that miracles ceased with the early church—that they are no longer relevant or necessary today.

One of the major reasons why many Christians, including pastors and leaders, refuse to accept the validity of miracles today is that they have failed to understand their importance. They do not have a revelation of God's *purposes* for manifesting His supernatural power. His purposes are to…

- prove He is the only true and living God.
- bring glory and honor to His name.
- confirm His Word.
- instill a reverential fear of Himself in the hearts of His people.
- deliver His people out of the hands of their enemies.
- supernaturally provide for His people.
- distinguish and set apart His people from those of the world.
- fulfill prophecy.
- warn of coming judgment upon unbelievers.
- bring in the great end-time harvest.

Another reason believers reject miracles is that Satan tries to deceive people into believing God's supernatural power is unnecessary because he does not want his destructive plans for the earth to be thwarted. He will do anything to discredit or hinder the flow of the miraculous manifested in Jesus' name. Yet, like Peter, John, and the other disciples in the early church, we must not be deterred from walking in the supernatural by any intimidation or threats we face by the religious establishment, by the enemy, or by the world.

To illustrate, let's go on a spiritual journey, back in time, to approximately AD 30, where Peter and John were standing before the religious rulers of their day—the high priest, elders, and scribes—to give an account of the miraculous healing of the lame man manifested through Peter in Jesus' name. (See Acts 3–4.)

It had been just two or three weeks since Christ met with His followers one last time on the Mount of Olives and gave them their final charge before ascending to heaven. On Pentecost, under the awesome influence of the baptism in the Holy Spirit, Peter preached about Jesus, and three thousand people were saved. Later, possibly the following day, Peter and John went to the temple at the hour of prayer. As they were going through the gate into the

> **To confirm His Word and provide for His people, God manifests His supernatural power.**

temple, they saw a man lying on the side of the road begging for alms. We know that he had been lame from birth and that he was over forty years old. We also know that he had been laid daily at the gate, though we do not know for how many of those years he had been brought there.

One thing is certain: that day was the lame man's day for a miracle!

His day probably began like every other. He saw two men going into the temple and asked them for money. He wasn't expecting anything unusual. If he was fortunate, he would get a few denari to help him through the day. The lame man didn't realize he was asking for help at the beginning of a new era of the supernatural manifestation of God flowing through His church.

Peter remembered the words Jesus had spoken, *"You shall receive power when the Holy Spirit has come upon you"* (Acts 1:8). The tongues of fire had been manifested over Peter's head at Pentecost. He had heard the sound of the rushing, mighty wind as God had breathed the Holy Spirit upon the believers. When he saw the man, he knew what to do. Unlike the vast majority of Christians today who see the blind, lame, and diseased and feel powerless to do anything, Peter *acted* on the promise He had received from Christ.

Peter knew he had received power, and Jesus had told His followers they would do the same works He had done, in His name. He therefore fixed his gaze upon the man and told him, *"Look at us"* (Acts 3:4). He wanted the lame man to look him in the face because he had the fire of God inside and wanted to release God's miracle power to bring healing to him.

The lame man looked up and stretched out his hand to receive alms. But Peter took him by the hand and said, *"Silver and gold I do not have, but what I do have I give you: In the name of Jesus Christ of Nazareth, rise up and walk"* (Acts 3:6).

Peter didn't pray a long, drawn-out prayer. He didn't doubt or hesitate. He took the man's hand and lifted him to his feet, and God's miracle power was manifested in Jesus' name. A surge of God's power coursed through the man's body, down his legs to his ankles. He began walking, leaping, and praising God as he went with Peter and John into the temple!

ARE YOU READY TO WALK IN THE SUPERNATURAL?

When the people saw what had happened to the lame man, a crowd gathered at Solomon's porch. Seizing the moment, Peter began to preach Jesus and explained the miracle power that had been released through His name. *"And His name, through faith in His name, has made this man strong, whom you see and know. Yes, the faith which comes through Him has given him this perfect soundness in the presence of you all"* (Acts 3:16).

This miracle, manifested in Jesus' name, shook the town, and five thousand men, not counting women and children, were added to the church that day.

That one miracle shook the religious establishment. The priests, captain of the temple, and Sadducees came running up to find out what was going on. Instead of recognizing the miracle that had taken place and glorifying God, they threw Peter and John in jail. The following day, they brought Peter and John before the religious establishment to give an account of this tremendous miracle. They had seen the response of the people and the thousands who had believed and accepted Christ. They felt threatened and no doubt thought they would lose their position—and the hold they had on the people.

Annas, the high priest, Caiaphas, John, Alexander, and all of Annas's relatives were there to determine by what power Peter and John had performed this miracle. It is important to note that, at the very inception of the church, Satan was working through the religious leaders to try to stop the preaching, teaching, and working of miracles in Jesus' name.

The leaders could not deny that a great miracle had taken place in the life of the former lame man. All of Jerusalem knew of his amazing healing. He was living proof of the supernatural power of God released in the name of Jesus. Yet the religious leaders were focused on one thing: they were determined to stop the flow of the supernatural power of God. Peter and John made clear what was the Source of the power that had healed the man. When the religious leaders asked them, *"By what power or by what name have you done this?"* (Acts 4:7), Peter boldly declared, *"By the name of Jesus Christ of Nazareth, whom you crucified, whom God raised from the dead, by Him this man stands here before you whole"* (v. 10).

> **If the disciples had denied God's miracle power, the church would have been spiritually short-circuited.**

It was by the name of Jesus that the supernatural, miracle-working power was manifested through the church to the world. When the high priest and the rest of the council could not find sufficient reason to punish Peter and John, they decided to use threats and intimidation to stop them from spreading the gospel. They commanded them not to preach or teach anymore in Jesus' name.

This was a defining moment—a turning point—for the early church.

They had a choice: to obey the religious leaders or to obey God and continue to proclaim salvation, healing, and deliverance in Jesus' name.

They had a choice: to compromise the Word and deny the miracle power of God they had received or to heal the sick, cast out demons, raise the dead, and do all the works Jesus promised they would do.

They had a choice: to preach a watered-down version of the gospel that would be acceptable to the religious leaders and the majority of the people or to boldly proclaim the truth of the gospel with signs following.

We know the choice they made. Peter and John said, *"For we cannot but speak the things which we have seen and heard"* (Acts 4:20). They were saying, in effect, "There is a supernatural power inside us we've never known before. This power cannot be quenched. It is alive, burning inside us, and it is impossible for us to be quiet or to quench the Spirit!"

The reaction and response of Peter, John, and the rest of the disciples to this satanic opposition through the religious leaders was absolutely critical at this point. Had they compromised, limited, or denied the miracle power of God and failed to proclaim the gospel in Jesus' name with signs following, the church would have been spiritually short-circuited before really beginning to fulfill its purpose.

Consider the consequences of their response if they had listened to and acted according to the threats and intimidation of the religious leaders. Where would the church be today if Peter and John had returned to the other disciples and essentially said, "Brothers, the religious leaders have threatened and commanded us not to preach or teach in Jesus' name. We must watch what we say. We must be 'politically correct' and not offend anyone. We don't want to ruffle anyone's feathers or do anything that would cause the religious leaders to come against us. When you pray for the sick or cast out demons, do it discreetly, behind closed doors. Be careful not to draw any attention to the fact that you believe in the miracle power of God and the power of Jesus' name."

Yet Peter and John broke through the opposition. They refused to be intimidated, discouraged, or defeated; they returned to their fellow believers and told them what had happened. Then they all lifted their voices in this united prayer:

Now, Lord, look on their threats, and grant to Your servants that with all boldness they may speak Your word, by stretching out Your hand to heal, and that signs and wonders may be done through the name of Your holy Servant Jesus.

(Acts 4:29–30)

The Scripture tells us that immediately following this prayer,

…the place where they were assembled together was shaken; and they were all filled with the Holy Spirit, and they spoke the word of God with boldness. (v. 31)

In their prayer, the believers asked God for three major things:

1. That they would have boldness to proclaim His Word.
2. That He would stretch forth His healing hand.
3. That signs and wonders would be done in the name of Jesus.

Notice that they did not whine and complain to God about the persecution they faced. They did not ask for God's intervention to stop the opposition. They asked for a holy boldness that would enable them to overcome in the midst of persecution and for the manifestation of miracles, signs, and wonders in Jesus' name as their credentials.

WHAT HAS HAPPENED TO THE TWENTY-FIRST CENTURY CHURCH?

The church of Jesus Christ experienced its greatest growth during its first three centuries. It was able to preach the gospel to the entire known world at that time without the aid of large sanctuaries and cathedrals, organized programs, or modern technology.

The early disciples weren't afraid to let go of the old rituals, the old forms of worship and formalism of the past, and allow the Holy Spirit to effect radical changes in their lives and in the world. They didn't place limits on the miracle power of God flowing through them but positioned themselves spiritually where the Holy Spirit could flow through them unhindered.

> **The early disciples positioned themselves spiritually where the Holy Spirit could flow through them unhindered.**

What has happened to the living, moving body of believers that was born in an explosion of power? What has happened to the manifestation of the miraculous in our churches? We build beautiful edifices, establish all types of programs, and develop high-tech, sophisticated ministries, but, on the whole, the supernatural, miracle power of God is missing.

When was the last time you witnessed a miracle in your church? Can you remember the last time God manifested His miracle power through *you*?

The church has lost the vision of what God intended it to be.

The apostle Paul warned that, in the last days, there would be people with *"a form of godliness but denying its power"* (2 Timothy 3:5). Could it be that we have become like the self-satisfied, lukewarm, Laodicean church that Christ rebuked and called to repentance in the book of Revelation? (See Revelation 3:14–22.)

Church, it is time to wake up! We have become sluggish and sleepy. We haven't been able to see our true condition. Jesus said, *"Anoint your eyes with eye salve, that you may see....Be zealous and repent"* (Revelation 3:18–19).

The miracle power of God has not changed—*we* have changed.

Our eyes have been diverted.

Our unity has been broken.

Our fervor and zeal have been diminished.

God never intended the immeasurable power of the Holy Spirit to be limited or contained within the four walls of what we call churches today. He never intended born-again Christians to sit contentedly on their comfortable pews, soaking up the blessings of God but never stepping out in faith and allowing the miracle power of God to flow through them to people around them who are in desperate need. He never intended the church to be fragmented, split by denominationalism or man-made philosophies or traditions. Never!

Jesus does not intend His church to know any limits but to operate in the same fullness of power that He did while He lived on the earth. He intends us to proclaim the gospel in a demonstration of the Spirit and power with signs following—healing the sick, casting out demons, and setting the oppressed free.

Just before Jesus ascended to heaven, He told His disciples: *"All authority has been given to Me in heaven and on earth. Go therefore and make disciples of all the nations, baptizing them in the name of the Father and of the Son and of the Holy Spirit"* (Matthew 28:18–19). Previously, He had said, *"Behold, I give you the authority to trample on serpents and scorpions, and over all the power of the enemy, and nothing shall by any means hurt you"* (Luke 10:19). Satan's power has been broken. He is not in control. Jesus has given the church all power and authority over him. We may have difficult times and trials, but we can overcome in the power of the Spirit.

From the moment God poured out the Holy Spirit on the one hundred twenty at Pentecost, the believers began to live in a new supernatural dimension of the Spirit. Miracles were expected, and they *accompanied* the preaching of the gospel. The disciples walked in the power of almighty God. *"Many wonders and signs were done through the apostles"* (Acts 2:43).

Could the lack of this ministry in the twenty-first-century church lie in the weakness of our relationship with the Lord and of our walking in the Spirit?

THE TWENTY-FIRST CENTURY CHURCH HAS A CHOICE

Just as the first-century church had a defining moment regarding whom they would serve, the twenty-first century church has reached a similar turning point.

We have a choice.

We can go along with the flow, compromise the Word, preach a watered-down version of the gospel, and deny the supernatural, miracle-working power of God. Or we can take a bold stand, acknowledging that God's miracle power is not only relevant, but also necessary today, and proclaim the truth of the gospel with signs following.

Many pastors of "seeker-friendly" churches are fearful of offending people and losing attendance at their churches, and therefore they will not allow the gifts of the Spirit to be manifested in their services. Other pastors, who are operating more in the flesh than in the Spirit, deny the power of God through their failure to pray for the sick and to deliver people from demonic power. Some Christian leaders are more concerned about being politically correct than they are about having the power and presence of almighty God in their services. They are afraid they will lose their social standing and influence in the community.

> **Some Christian leaders are more concerned about being politically correct than about having the presence of almighty God in their services.**

We cannot afford to continue denying the supernatural, miracle power of God. When the Israelites were defeated, it was not because the power of their enemies was greater, but because *"they turned back and tempted God, and limited the Holy One of Israel"* (Psalm 78:41 KJV). How did they limit God? They forgot the awesome manifestation of miracles, signs, and wonders He had worked on their behalf. They *"forgot His works and His wonders that He had shown them"* (v. 11).

- They forgot how He caused the Red Sea to part, allowing them to walk across on dry land.

- They forgot how He manifested His glory and led them through the wilderness with a cloud by day and fire by night.
- They forgot how He fed them manna from heaven and caused streams of water to gush forth out of rocks to quench their thirst.
- They denied His power and complained He had forsaken them.

After all His mighty works, they broke their covenant with Him. *"In spite of this they still sinned, and did not believe in His wondrous works"* (Psalm 78:32).

When God established His covenant with the Israelites, He commanded them not to forget Him and His ways but to teach His law and tell of His mighty works from generation to generation. The psalmist declared,

We will not hide them from their children, telling to the generation to come the praises of the LORD, and His strength and His wonderful works that He has done. (Psalm 78:4)

That the generation to come might know them, the children who would be born, that they may arise and declare them to their children. (v. 6)

God wanted to bless and prosper the people of Israel above all other peoples upon the face of the earth. But they forgot His marvelous works and continued to sin against Him. In the church today, we dare not fall into Satan's trap of ignoring or denying the reality and relevancy of the miracle power of God.

God did not send forth the third person of the Trinity, the Holy Spirit, in a demonstration and manifestation of power so that His church would be weak, anemic, and under the enemy's power. How has the church gotten so far away from God's original purpose for its ministry?

Jesus empowered and equipped the church so we would be able to set people free from the bondage of Satan, to loose them from their infirmities and meet the desperate needs in their lives. He infused the church with the power of the Holy Spirit so we would be able to carry on the same ministry He had on the earth. Through the power of the Holy Spirit operating in our lives, Christ intends us to do the same works He did—and greater. It is time for us to begin to do those greater works in the power and authority of His name.

GOD IS RAISING UP A HOLY REMNANT

God has always had a remnant of people through whom He could manifest His power and glory to the world. Throughout the years, God has raised up men and women—ordinary people like you and me—and baptized them with the Holy Spirit, giving them power and authority to work miracles in the name of Jesus.

Although God has raised up and anointed men and women with great ministries of healing and deliverance and used them mightily in manifesting miracles throughout the nations of the world, we must remember that He did not intend only a few select individuals to manifest His supernatural power. He planned that the entire body of Christ—especially His end-time people—would be infused with His power and authority to manifest miracles. He has called and chosen you to be a living witness, to give visible proof that Jesus is the Son of God.

We cannot deny the working of miracles or relegate them to the past. Don't listen to Satan's lies that you are just an insignificant person, and that you cannot do the same miraculous works that Jesus did. Jesus said, *"He who believes in Me, the works that I do he will do also; and greater works than these he will do, because I go to My Father"* (John 14:12).

Who are you going to believe?

Moses was an insignificant shepherd out in the wilderness when God called to him out of the burning bush, commissioned him for His purposes, and equipped him with signs and wonders as his credentials.

God has also called you and given you a Great Commission to fulfill. He has set you apart as His child and distinguished you from all other people in the world, with signs and wonders as your credentials.

> **God has given you the all-powerful name of Jesus, which gives you the authority to manifest His miracle power.**

Moses' rod was just a piece of wood that was made into a shepherd's tool. Yet it was symbolic of the supernatural power and authority God had placed in Moses' hands to perform miracles.

Similarly, God has placed His divine rod in your hands. He has given you the all-powerful name of Jesus, which gives you the authority to manifest His miracle power. Just as Moses picked up the rod of God and used it to perform miracles and fulfill the commission God had given him, you must begin to release God's miracle power in the name of Jesus and use it to fulfill the commission He has given you.

As we enter this new dimension of the supernatural, the Word will be preached by the church in an amazing demonstration of God's miracle-working power. God will use the body of Christ, a holy end-time remnant, to manifest His life and bring salvation and deliverance to the world as a final witness before Jesus' return.

- The blind will see.
- The lame will walk.
- Demons will be cast out.
- The Word of God will increase and will harvest a multitude of souls from around the world.

We will not just be *talking* about God's miracle power to save, heal, and deliver from drugs, alcohol, greed, unforgiveness, and all the power of the enemy. God will *confirm* what we say with signs following!

PERSONAL APPLICATION

1. In prayer, search your heart and mind to see if there are any teachings, doctrines, thoughts, doubt, fear, or unbelief that are hindering you from believing God will work a miracle in your life or will release His miracle power through you.

2. To help you with the above, ask yourself the following questions, then write down your responses:

   - What have I been taught concerning miracles?

   - Do I believe God still manifests His miracle power and that miracles are for today? (If so, write down why you believe.)

   - When I face what seem to be impossible circumstances, do I believe and expect God to work a miracle on my behalf, or do I rely on my natural mind—my natural wisdom and solutions?

   - In the problems and circumstances I am currently facing, am I believing and expecting God to perform a miracle?

   - Have I focused my thoughts on God's promises concerning His miracle provision in my life?

   - Am I speaking faith-filled words or am I living according to my natural senses—what I see, hear, or feel?

   - Have I developed a preconceived idea of how, when, and where I want God to manifest His miracle power in my circumstances?

- Do I believe God will release His miracle power through me to minister healing and deliverance to others in Jesus' name?

Record your answers on a sheet of paper or in a journal. Ask your heavenly Father to open your spiritual understanding so you will see how He wants to release His miracle power through you in ministering to the needs around you. Get rid of every hindrance by renewing your mind to the truth revealed in God's Word.

3. When the disciples in the early church were threatened and commanded not to preach or teach in Jesus' name, they did not hide or retreat. They refused to remain silent but united together in prayer. (See Acts 4:29–30.) In this prayer, they asked for three major things:

   - That they would have boldness to proclaim God's Word.
   - That He would stretch forth His healing hand.
   - That signs and wonders would be done in the name of Jesus.

Make a decision that you will not deny the supernatural power of God or limit the flow of miracles in your life. Then, begin to earnestly seek God for these three things to be manifested. Make the prayer of the early church the prayer of your heart. Ask God to give you boldness to share your faith with others wherever you are—at home, on the job, at school, in your neigh-borhood. Take every possible opportunity God opens up for you to pray for those in need, believing that God's healing power will flow through you.

CHAPTER FOUR

POSITIONING YOURSELF FOR THE SUPERNATURAL

It is one thing to believe that God is bringing the church into a new supernatural dimension of His power and to believe He will release miracles, signs, and wonders greater than anything we have seen or experienced. It is quite another to be a vital part of this coming great move of God and experience His miracle power flowing in your life, your family, your job, and your community.

You must *position yourself* to take hold of God's miracle power. This is not something that will just happen automatically. You must rid yourself of all traces of unbelief and prepare your heart through intimate communion with the Lord and by aligning your mind with His Word.

REVELATION PRECEDES MANIFESTATION

One of the major reasons why so many Christians within the body of Christ refuse to accept the validity of miracles today and fail to believe that God still works miracles on behalf of His people is a lack of revelation knowledge. Before a person can receive a miracle or be used to work miracles in Jesus' name, he must first have a revelation of God the Father in His power and glory, and a revelation of his personal calling to manifest that power and glory to the world.

Revelation knowledge goes beyond mere head knowledge. True revelation is born of the Spirit. It is wonderful to study the Word and acquire knowledge concerning the miraculous power of God. But until the Holy Spirit lifts the veil of darkness from our eyes and illuminates our spirits, we will not truly believe in it or act on it.

> To live in the supernatural, you must receive what God has revealed through His Word.

The apostle Peter lived in close communion with Jesus. He observed Jesus' miracles. He watched blind eyes being opened and saw the power of God flowing through Him to cast out demons and raise the dead. But one day Peter had a revelation. He told Jesus, *"You are the Christ, the Son of the living God"* (Matthew 16:16). Jesus answered, *"Blessed are you, Simon Bar-Jonah, for flesh and blood has not revealed this to you, but My Father who is in heaven"* (v. 17).

Spiritual things, including the supernatural power of God, cannot be understood through logic or man's natural understanding. No matter how hard a person may try, he cannot comprehend or accept them. In fact, they can even seem foolish to him. *"The natural man does not receive the things of the Spirit of God, for they are foolishness to him; nor can he know them, because they are spiritually discerned"* (1 Corinthians 2:14).

The only way a person can know all the wonderful things God has for him is through *revelation* received by the Holy Spirit. Paul wrote,

> *As it is written: "Eye has not seen, nor ear heard, nor have entered into the heart of man the things which God has prepared for those who love Him." But God has revealed them to us through His Spirit. For the Spirit searches all things, yes, the deep things of God.* (1 Corinthians 2:9–10)

To live in the supernatural and experience God's miracle power in your life, therefore, you must receive what God has revealed through His Word, asking the Holy Spirit to illuminate your heart and mind to His truth.

FOUR KEYS TO RECEIVING REVELATION OF THE SUPERNATURAL

Throughout the Bible, there are many powerful truths that reveal it is God's will for His people not only to experience His supernatural power, but also to live a supernatural life, empowered by His Spirit. The following are four keys to receiving revelation knowledge of the supernatural that will give you a strong foundation for walking in the power of God.

1. KNOW THAT GOD HAS PLANNED FOR YOU TO WALK IN THE MIRACULOUS.

From His very first dealings with the Israelites to His relationship today with the church on earth, the Father's intent has been to set apart for Himself a people on whom to bestow His blessings and favor. When the Israelites were in the wilderness, He revealed Himself as the God of supernatural provision, and He provided for all their spiritual, emotional, and physical needs.

On Mt. Sinai, God entered into a covenant with Israel and promised,

> *Now it shall come to pass, if you diligently obey the voice of the LORD your God, to observe carefully all His commandments which I command you today, that the LORD your God will set you high above all nations of the earth.*
>
> *(Deuteronomy 28:1)*

The children of Israel were marked for God's appointed blessings. In Deuteronomy 28, He promised,

> *Blessed shall you be in the city, and blessed shall you be in the country.* (v. 3)

> *Blessed shall you be when you come in, and blessed shall you be when you go out.* (v. 6)

> *The LORD will cause your enemies who rise against you to be defeated before your face; they shall come out against you one way and flee before you seven ways.* (v. 7)

> *The LORD will command the blessing on you in your storehouses and in all to which you set your hand, and He will bless you in the land which the LORD your God is giving you.* (v. 8)

> *The LORD will open to you His good treasure, the heavens, to give the rain to your land in its season, and to bless all the work of your hand. You shall lend to many nations, but you shall not borrow.* (v. 12)

And the LORD will make you the head and not the tail; you shall be above only, and not be beneath, if you heed the commandments of the LORD your God, which I command you today, and are careful to observe them. (v. 13)

When the Israelites' forty years in the wilderness were over, God anointed Joshua to lead a new generation into a new season of taking possession of His promised blessings. The surrounding nations saw that God's hand was upon His people. They observed how He supernaturally delivered their enemies into their hands. They saw His multiplied blessings upon their lives and everything they possessed. The Gentile nations saw and trembled because, as God's chosen people served the living God, He supernaturally manifested Himself on their behalf and poured out His blessings upon them.

> **God is calling forth a new breed of people through whom He can manifest His power and glory.**

Today is a new season for God's anointed, chosen people—His church. We, too, are a marked generation. He is calling forth a holy, prophetic generation—a new breed of people through whom He will manifest His power and glory as a witness to the world that He is God Almighty and there is none other.

This is the season when God will manifest Himself among His chosen people in supernatural provision and blessing to the world. The Father desires to bring His chosen sons and daughters into a strong covenant relationship with Him that will open the windows of heaven and release His supernatural blessings and provision.

He desires for you to live with a daily expectancy of miracles in your life and circumstances. He has provided a way for you to have direct access to Him, where all things are possible (see Matthew 19:26), where all your needs can be met (see Philippians 4:19), and where you can receive *anything* by asking in Jesus' name. Jesus promised, *"And whatever you ask in My name, that I will do, that the Father may be glorified in the Son. If you ask anything in My name, I will do it"* (John 14:13–14).

Are you ready to receive?

2. RELINQUISH ALL CLAIMS TO YOUR LIFE

If you are to have the supernatural, miracle power of God, you must relinquish all claims to your life and be willing to lose your life for Christ's sake. Christ's purpose for His church is that we grow to full maturity, *"to a perfect man, to the measure of the stature of the fullness of Christ"* (Ephesians 4:13).

In the past few years, I believe there has been an acceleration of this maturing process in the lives of many believers. We have reached a season in this end-time hour before Christ's return where the Father is bringing His sons and daughters into full growth, into the full stature of Jesus Christ. This maturing is taking place from one degree of glory to another. (See 2 Corinthians 3:18.)

I am not talking about what we see today in the experience of the average Christian. I am talking about a revolutionary new type of Christian who has had a revelation of God's purpose for his life and who has totally yielded himself to allow the Holy Spirit to change and transform him into Christ's likeness. I am referring to radical Christianity.

The transformation process cannot be accomplished by your own human efforts, but only by His Spirit living in you. It will take place in your life according to the degree you are willing to die to yourself, and to the extent you are yielded to His will and ready for God to change you. Jesus said,

If anyone desires to come after Me, let him deny himself, and take up his cross, and follow Me. (Matthew 16:24)

Unless a grain of wheat falls into the ground and dies, it remains alone; but if it dies, it produces much grain. He who loves his life will lose it, and he who hates his life in this world will keep it for eternal life. (John 12:24–25)

When Jesus came to earth, He stripped Himself of His divine attributes and was born in the likeness of men (see Philippians 2:5–8), was anointed by the Holy Spirit (see Acts 10:38), lived a sinless life (see Hebrews 4:15), healed the sick (see Matthew 4:23), and defeated Satan (see Acts 10:38)—leaving us an example to follow.

> As Jesus was the express image of God, it is possible for you to be the express image of Christ.

Too long, we have settled for a weak, powerless, lukewarm, defeated Christianity. God has planned for His sons and daughters to think, talk, and act as Jesus did. He intends for us to rise up in full maturity to do the same works as Jesus did in the same power and anointing of His Holy Spirit.

How hungry are you to live your life in the power and anointing of the Holy Spirit, as Jesus did?

Are you truly ready and willing to say, "Whatever it takes"?

Are you ready to give up yourself? Are you willing to crucify your sinful nature? Are you willing to give God your personal goals, ambitions, and dreams? Are you willing to humble yourself and acknowledge your total dependence upon Him?

Denying yourself is not for the weak or fainthearted. It isn't easy to die. It is painful. It cost Jesus everything to submit to the heavenly Father in fulfillment of His purpose, and it will cost you everything if you want to fulfill your purpose and walk in the same kind of power and anointing.

From the beginning of time, God the Father planned that Christ, through His death and resurrection, would be the firstborn of many spiritually reborn sons and daughters who would bear the image of their Elder Brother, and who would become joint-heirs with Him.

For whom he did foreknow, he also did predestinate to be conformed to the image of his Son, that he might be the first-born among many brethren. (Romans 8:29)

Christ's life on earth as the Son of God is a revelation, an exact pattern, of what God's sons and daughters are to be today. Jesus came to show us what it is like to live a life devoted to God. As Jesus was the express image of God, it is possible for you to be the express image of Christ. As Jesus was a visible representation and manifestation of God to people on earth, you can be a visible representation and manifestation of Christ to people on earth today.

You may look at your life, with all your human limitations, and wonder how you can be changed into Christ's image, whereby the supernatural life of God can flow out of you as it flowed out of Jesus, healing the sick, casting out demons, and setting the oppressed free. The word *"conformed"* in Romans 8:29 is translated from a Greek word meaning "to bring to the same outward expression as something else." You can be assured that God has planned for you to be brought to the same outward expression of Jesus: *"As He is, so are we in this world"* (1 John 4:17).

Because of His obedience, even unto death, Christ was exalted and restored to the glory He had with the Father before He came to earth. (See Philippians 2:9–10.) He is seated in a position of supreme power and glory, *"far above all principality and power and might and dominion, and every name that is named, not only in this age but also in that which is to come"* (Ephesians 1:21). The Father purposes to bring *"many sons to glory"* (see Hebrews 2:10). He intends that same glory to radiate from your being!

> *And all of us, as with unveiled face, [because we] continued to behold [in the Word of God] as in a mirror the glory of the Lord, are constantly being transfigured into His very own image in ever increasing splendor and from one degree of glory to another; [for this comes] from the Lord [Who is] the Spirit.* (2 Corinthians 3:18 AMP)

It is not your physical features that are being changed into an exact image of Christ as a son or daughter of God; you are carrying around the glory of God in your spirit.

Make no mistake. Satan wants to stunt your spiritual growth and hinder you from reaching full maturity. He doesn't want you to surrender your life to God or to come into a full revelation of who you are in Jesus Christ. He wants you to settle for less than what Christ has made possible. He wants you to keep your eyes focused on your human limitations.

For too long we have brought the Word of God down to the level of our experience, instead of bringing the level of our experience up to meet the Word. You must therefore know that…

- God has begotten you by His Spirit. (See John 1:12–13.)
- God has birthed the life of Christ, the all-powerful Son of God, within you. (See Galatians 4:4–7.)
- the fullness of the Godhead lives in you. (See Colossians 2:9–10.)
- you are a partaker of God's divine nature. (See 2 Peter 1:4.)
- you are a joint-heir with Jesus. (See Romans 8:16–17.)

Having a spiritual awareness that you are a child of God, and that He intends for you to be changed into Christ's image as you yield to Him—with His life flowing out of you in a manifestation of power and glory—is a prerequisite to walking in the supernatural.

3. KNOW YOUR POSITION OF KINGDOM DOMINION AND WALK IN IT

To walk in the supernatural, you must also understand that God intends His people to take kingdom dominion on earth. From the very beginning, even before He created man, He purposed that humanity would rule over creation:

Then God said, "Let Us make man in Our image, according to Our likeness; let them have dominion over the fish of the sea, over the birds of the air, and over the cattle, over all the earth and over every creeping thing that creeps on the earth." (Genesis 1:26)

The Father said He wanted humanity to have *dominion*. He formed man, placed him on earth, and exalted him by giving him the ability to subdue and rule over the created world. He told Adam and Eve, *"Be fruitful and multiply; fill the earth and subdue it; have dominion over the fish of the sea, over the birds of the air, and over every living thing that moves on the earth"* (Genesis 1:28).

In this verse, the word *"subdue"* is taken from the Hebrew root word *kabash*, meaning "to trample underfoot—to conquer." Generally speaking, the word *subdue* is a military term meaning "to bring into subjection." The word *"dominion"* is taken from the Hebrew word *radah*, which means "to rule over." Together, these two words paint a picture of humanity's total dominion over the earth.

> From the very beginning, even before He created man, God purposed that humanity would rule over creation.

Adam and Eve, through their rebellion against God, forfeited humanity's position of power, authority, and dominion. Jesus came to earth to redeem human beings and restore our position of power and dominion. He came to destroy all the works of the devil—sin, sickness, and death. He came to establish God's kingdom on earth and to restore and elevate man to an even greater position of power and authority than Adam and Eve originally had.

Note that when Jesus sent His twelve disciples out to minister, He said, *"And as you go, preach, saying, 'The kingdom of heaven is at hand.' Heal the sick, cleanse the lepers, raise the dead, cast out demons. Freely you have received, freely give"* (Matthew 10:7–8). Then, when Jesus was preparing to go to the cross, He told His disciples that believers would have the same power, authority, and dominion to do the works He had done. This includes...

- healing the sick.
- casting out demons.
- raising the dead.

Jesus said, *"Most assuredly, I say to you, he who believes in Me, the works that I do he will do also; and greater works than these he will do, because I go to My Father"* (John 14:12). Think of it—through Jesus' life, death, and resurrection, you have been elevated to an even greater position of power, authority, and dominion than that of Adam or the Old Testament prophets. By His Spirit, God has made you one of His sons or daughters, and He intends for you to bring His light and life to your community, city, and nation.

Are you ready?

4. TAKE YOUR POSITION OF POWER AND AUTHORITY OVER SATAN

To walk in the supernatural, you must not only know who you are in Christ, and that you have dominion over the earth. You must also know your position of power and authority over

Satan, and you must exercise that power. As God brings the church into this new dimension of His miraculous power, He will raise up men and women who are full of the anointing of the Holy Spirit. Men and women who...

- know the power and deceit of the enemy.
- know their position of God-given spiritual power.
- are not afraid to confront Satan and take authority over him in Jesus' name.

For hundreds of years, Christians have sat back with their hands folded while Satan has infested the earth with every form of sin and sickness imaginable. Christians have been deceived into thinking they are little, insignificant "worms" who have no control over the sin, sickness, or death surrounding them. Very few believers fully understand their position of power over the enemy, and even fewer have been willing to step out in faith to use that power.

The call of the Spirit today is for Christians to know their God-given position and, through the supernatural power of almighty God flowing through them, take authority and dominion over Satan and his evil principalities to establish God's will and kingdom on earth.

I have experienced the manifestation of this call firsthand. A young lady had been persuaded by others, who were deeply concerned about her physical and spiritual welfare, to attend one of our Deliverance Crusades in Georgia, despite the fact that she mocked and talked against the meetings. When the altar call was given, the same people who had encouraged her to attend were instrumental in getting her to come forward.

Altar workers took her to the prayer room, where a demon within her began to exercise his authority over her. Her mouth suddenly closed like a trap, her fists clenched, her eyes bulged, and she turned deathly white. Then, all at once, she became violently wild and began to act like an untamed animal.

The people prayed for her, but she seemed to get worse. They sent for me where I was praying for those in the prayer line to be healed. As I drew near, the girl leered at me and cowered before me. It was obvious that the demon in that girl detected the Spirit of God in my life, just as the evil spirits in the demoniac at Gadara had discerned the presence of Jesus. (See Luke 8:26–35.)

> **Jesus has made it possible for you to exercise kingdom dominion.**

You can be sure, the devil and his demons know all who belong to God. In Acts 19, we read that certain Jewish exorcists tried their hand at using the name of the Lord Jesus on those possessed by demon spirits. They would say, *"We exorcise you by the Jesus whom Paul preaches"* (Acts 19:13). Seven sons of Sceva, a Jewish high priest, tried this method with a man who had an evil spirit, but the demon answered, *"Jesus I know, and Paul I know; but who are you?"* (v. 15). Then the man with the evil spirit overpowered them all and handled them with such violence they ran out of the house naked and battered. The demons knew and respected Jesus and His servant Paul because Jesus and Paul walked in the power of the Spirit. They also know and fear believers today who exercise the authority God has given them to *"cast out demons"* (Mark 16:17) in the name of Jesus.

Understanding this truth, I pushed toward the young lady, reached out, and grabbed one of her arms. I placed my hand on her head and breathed a prayer. I wasn't apprehensive because I knew deliverance was going to take place through the Holy Spirit. In such a situation, one must be confident that the Holy Spirit is present and will take over and do the miraculous.

As I prayed for the young woman, she became as calm and helpless as a child and fell to the floor. Suddenly a smile broke out on her face. She stood to her feet and began to exclaim how wonderfully happy she felt inside, and to thank the Lord for making her whole. She exclaimed, "Something *went out of me!*"

This incident may seem absurd or fantastic to some, but to that girl and to everyone else who has ever been possessed or even oppressed by demons, such a thing is a very real and terrifying experience. However, Jesus has all power in heaven and in earth, and He is always ready to deliver those who come to Him in repentance and with a willingness to forsake their sin and fleshly mind-set. And, He has made it possible for you to exercise kingdom dominion and authority to set free those who are bound by the powers of darkness.

A similar instance that stands out vividly in my mind was the healing of a demon-possessed woman during one of my meetings in the Dominican Republic. Shortly after she came to the service, she began to carry on. She was trying to tear her clothes off; she was foaming at the mouth, and she was uttering the most bloodcurdling screams. Even now, when I think of those awful screams, it makes me shudder.

The people who brought her to the meeting were very sincere and desperately wanted her to be delivered, so they brought her right up to the front where she could be prayed for. Several thousand people were in the meeting, and all eyes were focused on this terrible scene. It was as if the devil said to me, "T. L. Lowery, you have met your match tonight. If this woman isn't delivered and quieted, you are really going to look like a fool!"

I wasn't the least bit fearful. I said, "Yes, Satan, and when God does liberate this wretched soul, you are going to look worse than a fool." I knew God would fulfill His Word that night and prove His power before all those people.

The devil intended to ruin our service, but as always, the Lord turned the evil designs of the devil around to enhance His own glory. I laid my hands on the woman's head and began to pray. As I did, she went into raging convulsions and tried to tear off my clothes and scratch my face, but she was unable to harm me.

As I continued to pray, she seemed to get even more violent, and she began coughing and spitting up the foulest-smelling substance one could ever imagine. No wonder one of the names by which Satan is known is "Beelzebub." (See, for example, Mark 3:22.) This name is composed of two words: *Beel*, "master," and *zebub*, "of the flies." The term is therefore translated as "master of the flies," "master of the dung heap," "god of corruption," or "god of filth and pollution."

This name reveals very well an aspect of the nature and activities of Satan and his depraved agents. It helps us to understand why they delight in such things as the festering sores of Job, the putrid flesh of lepers, and the stink of cancers.

As the demons in this woman continued to act up in this way, I said to the Lord, "I am not asking that she be delivered for my interest but for Your glory. Your cause is at stake." At that moment, I began to pray in tongues, in a language that Satan cannot understand—a holy language in which there has never been uttered any cursing or blasphemy, but only praises to God. Thank the Lord for the Holy Spirit, because *"He makes intercession for the saints according to the will of God"* (Romans 8:27).

> God is our Source of supernatural supply for every area of our lives.

When the Holy Spirit began to pray through me in that manner, the woman just wilted to the floor, delivered and set free by the power of God. I have never seen a crowd of people more affected by what they saw than that one. It convinced them that God is real and that He will not let His children down.

Jesus intended the ability to cast out demons to be a vital part of the spiritual armor of all believers, saying, *"And these signs will follow those who believe: In My name they will cast out demons"* (Mark 16:17), and *"Behold, I give you the authority to trample on serpents and scorpions, and over all the power of the enemy"* (Luke 10:19). In this end-time hour, He is sending us forth to expose and cast out demons that have been unleashed by Satan. When we are filled with the Holy Spirit and command demons to leave in the name of Jesus, they recognize the power of God within us and must obey. They have no choice.

Exercising authority and casting out demons is therefore not something we should consider abnormal. What is abnormal is the fact that the great majority of Christians in our churches today have failed to take their position of power and authority over the demons that are attacking, oppressing, and tormenting people.

It is time for the church of Jesus Christ to cast out unbelief and get on our faces before God through prayer and fasting until we are so full of the power and anointing of the Holy Spirit that we will be able to fulfill the ministry of deliverance Christ intended. The Father will raise up those who are willing and fully yielded to Him as mighty warriors confronting the darkness, casting out demons, and setting the captives free wherever they go.

I believe there is coming such a powerful manifestation of God's Spirit within this radical new breed of Christians He is raising up, that demons will recognize we have power in the name of Jesus to bind the *"strong man"* (see, for example, Matthew 12:29), break their power, and cast them out. Just as people came to Jesus to be set free because they knew demons were powerless before Him, people will know God has a people who have the same anointing and power to set the oppressed free.

If you are going to walk in the supernatural, you must exercise your spiritual authority over Satan in the circumstances of your life, family, and ministry. Two thousand years ago, Jesus defeated Satan. (See, for example, Hebrews 2:14.) He came to destroy the works of the devil and set men free from his power. (See 1 John 3:8.) You have been given authority over all the power of the enemy. (See Luke 10:19.) In the name of Jesus, every demon in hell must obey.

ARE YOU READY?

Walking in the supernatural involves having a spiritual breakthrough whereby God opens our eyes so that we begin to look to Him as our Source of supernatural supply for every area of our lives—our health, our finances, our family circumstances, everything.

Are you ready for a fresh revelation of God as One who stands ready to supernaturally meet your needs? Are you ready to receive a revelation of God's supernatural power flowing through your life?

If your answer to these questions is yes, position yourself today to take hold of His miraculous provision now being released within the body of Christ.

Put your faith into action by implementing the four steps I have outlined in this chapter, and start walking in the supernatural.

PERSONAL APPLICATION

Put these four keys to walking in the supernatural power of God into practice in your daily life. Read them aloud every day, review the preceding sections explaining them, and act upon them in faith. Then, get ready for God's miracle power to flow through you.

- *Know* that God has planned for you to walk in the miraculous.
- Relinquish all claims to your life.
- Know your position of kingdom dominion and walk in it.
- Take your position of power and authority over Satan.

CHAPTER FIVE

BREAKING THROUGH TO THE SUPERNATURAL

Y ou were made for miracles, and miracles were made for you!

As we have seen, God created humanity through a supernatural manifestation of His power, and He intends to deal with His children today in a supernatural way. You may still be wondering, *If it is true that I was made for miracles and God desires to manifest His miraculous power in my circumstances, why haven't I been able to take hold of the miracles I need?*

To walk in the supernatural, you have to press through in the Spirit and break down every hindrance that stands in your way. You cannot walk in the flow of God's glory and power simply by wishing or desiring it. You must know how to break through to the supernatural where God's miracle power can be released *in* and *through* you.

BREAK THROUGH NATURAL LIMITATIONS

One of the biggest hindrances you will face in walking in the supernatural is your own natural living environment. By natural living environment, I mean both your limited human perspective and abilities, as well as your fallen human nature. Your personal living environment includes…

- your thoughts
- your imaginations
- your preconceived ideas
- your attitudes
- your emotions
- your circumstances
- what you see, hear, and speak

Each one of these areas can hinder you from receiving the miracle you need and stop you from experiencing a continual flow of God's miracle power. You must understand your own personal environment as it relates to miracles. Unless you are knowledgeable about your environment, there is no possible way you will be able to break through the natural barriers hindering you.

Since the fall of humanity in rebellion against God, our personal environments have been influenced, governed, or controlled by what the apostle Paul called the *"natural man"* (1 Corinthians 2:14), or the mind-set and motivations of humanity apart from God. Through Christ, we can *"live by the Spirit, and…not gratify the desires of the sinful nature"* (Galatians 5:16 NIV). Yet a great majority of Christians are still living in such a way that they are shaped or controlled by this nature, as well as by the limitations of the physical world. Most people go through life depending on their own abilities and natural minds, instead of depending on God's miraculous intervention, trusting Him to supernaturally provide.

The supernatural flow of God's miracle power—which will enable you to accomplish the greater works Jesus said you would do—cannot be manifested by your natural strivings. As long as you remain bound by the natural, it is impossible to walk in the supernatural and take hold of the miracles you need. Once you have broken through your natural limitations, however, you will be able to live in an atmosphere whereby you can experience miracles in every area of your life.

THE ENVIRONMENT OF SPIRIT, SOUL, AND BODY

The first thing we must understand about our natural environment is that human beings are comprised of spirit, soul, and body.

SPIRIT

The spirit is the essence of who we are as human beings. The Greek word for spirit is *pneuma*; its literal meaning is "breath." The spirit of man is the quality of life God gave to him in creation. God *"forms the spirit of man within him"* (Zechariah 12:1). The spirit is the life God first breathed into Adam, and it is the part of human beings whereby they are able to communicate with and worship Him. *"God is Spirit, and those who worship Him must worship in spirit and truth"* (John 4:24).

The spirit of fallen man is dead because of sin. But when we are born again, our spirits are regenerated, and the Holy Spirit comes to live within us. Paul told the believers in the Corinthian church, *"Don't you know that you yourselves are God's temple and that God's Spirit lives in you?"* (1 Corinthians 3:16 NIV). As Christians, we become the temple or dwelling place of the Holy Spirit. Our spirits are infused and empowered by almighty God, giving us the supernatural ability—power beyond our natural capability—to walk in His life, power, and glory. Paul said, *"But you are not in the flesh but in the Spirit, if indeed the Spirit of God dwells in you. Now if anyone does not have the Spirit of Christ, he is not His....For as many as are led by the Spirit of God, these are sons of God"* (Romans 8:9, 14).

When Christ comes to live in us by His Spirit, His very life is manifested within us. Therefore, we no longer have to be bound by a sinful nature or natural environment; we don't have to live according to the "old" man with its carnal mind any longer. Instead, we enter into a new dimension where we can live according to the Spirit within us.

> The same *dunamis,* miracle power that was manifested through Jesus is in you through the Holy Spirit.

To break through into the supernatural, therefore, so that we are living continually in the life and power of God, we must understand that our spirits are supernaturally empowered by the Holy Spirit. Paul prayed for the Ephesian believers, *"May He grant you out of the rich treasury of His glory to be strengthened and reinforced with mighty power in the inner man by the [Holy] Spirit [Himself indwelling your innermost being and personality]"* (Ephesians 3:16 AMP). This verse is translated in the King James Version as *"...to be strengthened with might by his Spirit in the inner man."* Paul also prayed that the believers in the Colossian church would be *"strengthened with all might, according to His glorious power, for all patience and longsuffering with joy"* (Colossians 1:11).

The word *"might"* in the above verses is translated from the Greek word *dunamis,* which refers to the same miracle-working power that is in Jesus. Think about it—the same *dunamis,* miracle power that was manifested through Jesus is in you as a result of His Spirit living and dwelling within you!

BODY

Another aspect of our natural environment is the body. As I wrote earlier, we are spiritual beings who dwell in physical bodies. Paul wrote, *"I have been crucified with Christ; it is no longer I who live, but Christ lives in me; and the life which I now live in the flesh I live by faith in the Son of God, who loved me and gave Himself for me"* (Galatians 2:20). Our essential being—our spirit—lives by faith in Christ Jesus as we go about our earthly lives in these "houses" of flesh and blood.

SOUL—MIND, WILL, AND EMOTIONS

The main aspect of our personal environment we will look at in this chapter is our souls. The soul is comprised of the mind, will, and emotions. Our minds process our thoughts and imaginations. The Greek word used to refer to the mind is *nous,* which describes the mental functions of perception, understanding, knowing, feeling, judging, and determining.

When we are born again, our minds are set free from the control of the fallen nature—with its worldly desires, emotions, and will—and also from Satan's control. Walking in the Spirit means you no longer are bound by the limitations of your natural mind, wisdom, and abilities. When you are living as God intended, your regenerated spirit is guided and empowered by the Holy Spirit, and your spirit rules over your soul.

Note that our old, sinful nature has not been altered—we have been given a *new* nature. Paul told the Corinthians, *"Therefore, if anyone is in Christ, he is a new creation; old things have passed away; behold, all things have become new"* (2 Corinthians 5:17). You have a new heart and a new mind with renewed attitudes and desires, and a renewed will. Yet you need to recognize that your old nature is still active, and it wars against your new nature. Paul wrote, *"In my inner being I delight in God's law; but I see another law at work in the members of my body, waging war against the law of my mind"* (Romans 7:22–23 NIV).

The mind of the old nature is in direct opposition to the mind of the new nature—to the will, thoughts, plans, and purposes of God. It is impossible for the old, carnal mind to be in submission to God. The extent to which a Christian is governed by his old mind is the extent to which he will live in defeat. Those who are carnally minded cannot walk in the supernatural. *"But the natural man does not receive the things of the Spirit of God, for they are foolishness to him; nor can he know them, because they are spiritually discerned"* (1 Corinthians 2:14).

> **To live and walk in the supernatural, you must live according to your new nature.**

Satan does not want us to live according to our new nature and the Spirit of God within us. He will do everything within his power to fill your mind with anxiety, fear, defeat, and discouragement concerning your circumstances—until you are weakened, depressed, frustrated, and filled with a sense of hopelessness and despair. He will try to oppress and weigh down your mind with heavy burdens and pressures until you are unable to break through the natural realm into the supernatural, where all things are possible with God. (See Matthew 19:26.)

To live and walk in the supernatural, you must live according to your new nature, which has been divinely charged and energized by the Holy Spirit.

> *Now we have received, not the spirit of the world, but the Spirit who is from God, that we might know the things that have been freely given to us by God.*
>
> (1 Corinthians 2:12)

LIVE ACCORDING TO THE MIND OF CHRIST

God has given you a new nature and placed the Holy Spirit within you so that your spirit can rule over your carnal mind and its fleshly appetites.

> *For "who has known the mind of the LORD that he may instruct Him?" But we have the mind of Christ.*
>
> (1 Corinthians 2:16)

By God's Spirit within you, you possess a supernatural ability to discern spiritual truths that are not according to man's wisdom or natural understanding, but God's. The Scriptures tell us, *"We have the mind of Christ."* You have the supernatural mind of Christ to guide your natural mind and will, enabling you to have His perspective on every circumstance of your life. However, having the mind of Christ *operating* in your life is not automatic. Simply because you have been born again and have been given a new nature does not mean that you are necessarily living according to the mind of Christ. Yet Jesus has broken the power of Satan over your mind so that it is possible to live in this way. The power of sin, which once ruled in your heart and mind, has been defeated. You are no longer a slave to your carnal nature and carnal mind.

To live according to the mind of Christ, you must continually take authority over your carnal nature, and a definitive change must take place in your mind. Paul told the Romans,

> *And do not be conformed to this world, but be **transformed** by the renewing of your mind, that you may prove what is that good and acceptable and perfect will of God.*
> (Romans 12:2, emphasis added)

The *"renewing,"* or "making new" of the mind that Paul referred to is the adjustment of all our thoughts to those of the mind of Christ. This requires a conscious effort on our part. It requires discipline. The mind of Christ includes His thoughts, will, and purposes. It is the vast *"depth of the riches both of the wisdom and knowledge of God"* (Romans 11:33). Christ's mind is revealed to us by His Word and His Spirit. As we fill our hearts and minds with His Word, trusting the Holy Spirit to illuminate it for us, and as we bring our minds into submission to His thoughts, will, purposes, and desires, we are transformed into Christ's image, and we have His mind.

There are Christians who claim to have the mind of Christ yet allow their hearts and minds to be governed by carnal thoughts, desires, and attitudes. They are still living their lives according to their limited natural minds, with their limited understanding. The apostle Paul told the Corinthians,

> *For to be carnally minded is death, but to be spiritually minded is life and peace. Because the carnal mind is enmity ["hostile" NIV] against God; for it is not subject to the law of God, nor indeed can be. So then, those who are in the flesh cannot please God.* (Romans 8:6–8)

The word *"minded"* in verse 6 is translated from the Greek word *phronema*, which refers to what is *in* the mind—the thought or object of thought. The word *"carnal"* in verse 7 is translated from the Greek word *sarkikos*, which means "sensual; controlled by the animal appetites; governed by nature, instead of by the Spirit of God."

A Christian who is "carnally minded" is thus one who has allowed his mind to be filled with the carnal thoughts and desires of his old nature and is living his life according to them. Again, it is impossible for the carnal mind to be in submission to God. The mind of Christ and the carnal mind are as irreconcilable as light and darkness. The carnal mind cannot comprehend the things of the Spirit, nor is it able to understand the supernatural power of God. It is hostile to it.

As long as you are governed and controlled by your carnal mind, therefore, you will be unable to take hold of God's

> **The renewing of your mind to the mind of Christ must be a *continual* process.**

miracle power. This is why your mind must be continually renewed by the Word. You must draw the line and settle forever that you will no longer be bound by your natural environment and that you are done with sin—that you will not allow it to have any place in your life whatsoever.

To do this, you must be willing to crucify—put to death—the lust of your flesh. (See Galatians 5:16.) The works of the flesh include your own selfish desires, ambitions, and goals. You must get rid of your carnal thoughts and intentions. You must die! Your will must be totally surrendered to God and your life totally consumed in fulfilling His will. You must, by His Spirit within you, take authority over every aspect of your heart and mind and bring it under subjection to the mind of Christ.

The renewing of your mind to the mind of Christ must be a *continual* process. As you fill your mind with a knowledge of Jesus and bring your heart and mind into submission to the Holy Spirit, you are being *"renewed in knowledge according to the image of Him who created* [you]" (Colossians 3:10). You are bringing your mind in alignment with the unchanging, powerful, life-giving force of God's Word. Unless this continual renewal of your mind is taking place, there is no way you will be able to break through into the supernatural.

Peter told the believers in the early church,

Therefore, since Christ suffered for us in the flesh, arm yourselves also with the same mind, for he who has suffered in the flesh has ceased from sin, that he no longer should live the rest of his time in the flesh for the lusts of men, but for the will of God. (1 Peter 4:1–2)

"Arming yourself" with the mind of Christ does not mean simply reading the Bible. It means daily saturating your mind with God's Word, filling your thoughts with it, and living in obedience to it. It means meditating on it until it becomes an integral part of your life—until your thoughts, desires, intentions, and purposes are aligned with the will of God.

Paul said, *"Be **renewed** in the spirit of your mind"* (Ephesians 4:23, emphasis added). Likewise, *renewal* does not refer to your natural abilities in retaining knowledge. It is not enough to have head knowledge of who you are in Christ and all that He has provided for you through His covenant. Being renewed in the *"spirit of your mind"* refers to the thoughts, attitudes, and desires being brought under the dominion and control of the Holy Spirit so that you can be in fellowship with Christ and can direct your energies toward pleasing God and fulfilling His will.

As long as you are renewing your mind and the Holy Spirit is controlling your life, you will *live* according to the Spirit and will *walk* in the supernatural. Not everyone professing to be a son of God is a true son of God. The apostle Paul said, *"But if any one does not possess the [Holy] Spirit of Christ, he is none of His [he does not belong to Christ, is not truly a child of God]....But all who are led by the Spirit of God are sons of God"* (Romans 8:9, 14 AMP). Here is the test: those who have the Holy Spirit dwelling within them and who are walking according to the Spirit, submitted to and directed by Him, are the true children of God. This is why we must break through every natural limitation and walk as true sons or daughters of God, manifesting His supernatural power.

BRING EVERY THOUGHT CAPTIVE TO THE OBEDIENCE OF CHRIST

Living according to the mind of Christ involves what the Bible describes as *"casting down imaginations"* and *"bringing into captivity every thought"*:

(For the weapons of our warfare are not carnal, but mighty through God to the pulling down of strong holds;) casting down imaginations, and every high thing that exalteth itself against the knowledge of God, and bringing into captivity every thought to the obedience of Christ.

(2 Corinthians 10:4–5 KJV)

> **People have to overcome their negative, fearful thought patterns in order to break into the supernatural.**

Your mind influences every other part of your being. It feeds the desires of your will and emotions. It affects the attitudes you develop and your imagination, or the mental pictures you formulate and dwell on.

The kinds of thought patterns you have developed over the years concerning miracles can hinder you. You are a product of your environment. Catholics, Baptists, and Pentecostals are all products of their respective environments. After a person has been taught something all his life, it is hard for him to break out of that mind-set.

People who have been taught all their lives that miracles were given only for the purpose of founding the church, and that miracles continued only as long as they were needed for that purpose, eventually ceasing altogether—or even that miraculous healings can be attributed to Satan—can't help having a difficult time believing in miracles today. And people who have developed negative or fearful thought patterns when they've experienced troubles and trials in life also have a challenge to overcome in order to break into the supernatural.

For a moment, let's focus on some of the thought patterns you may have developed when you have faced circumstances that could require a supernatural manifestation of God's power. When certain physical symptoms appear in your body, does your imagination run wild? Can you see yourself having cancer, heart disease, or some other fatal disease? If you presently have a physical illness, have any of the following thoughts crossed your mind?

- *Why has God brought this illness upon me?*
- *I don't think I'm ever going to improve.*
- *I think I'm getting worse.*
- *I don't think I have enough faith to be healed.*

If you are facing financial problems, do you ever think any of these thoughts?

- *I don't think we're going to have enough money to pay all our bills this month.*
- *We are so far in debt it looks as if we will never get out.*
- *We'll never have enough money.*

It is at these times that we especially need to remember Paul's instruction, *"Do not be conformed to this world, but be transformed by the renewing of your mind"* (Romans 12:2). You must bring every thought into captivity and place it under obedience to Christ. The moment negative thoughts of doubt, unbelief, fear, or worry come into your mind, recognize them as a tool Satan uses to block you from taking hold of your miracle. Cast those thoughts out in the name of Jesus and replace them with the Word of God.

Regardless of the circumstances you are facing, begin right now to break through your personal environment by allowing your mind—your thoughts, attitudes, and imaginations—to be transformed and conformed to the Word of God.

TEAR DOWN THE STRONGHOLD OF UNBELIEF

In terms of the natural environment of our minds, doubt and unbelief are major strongholds we must recognize and deal with in the power of the Holy Spirit. These mental assaults will shut you off from taking hold of the miraculous and walking in the supernatural. The reason the church has not seen and experienced God's miracle power on a greater scale is that we have limited Him through a lack of faith. Jesus Himself was limited in working mighty miracles because of the unbelief of the people in His hometown of Nazareth.

He did not do many mighty works there because of their unbelief. (Matthew 13:58)

He could do no mighty work there, except that He laid His hands on a few sick people and healed them. And He marveled because of their unbelief. Then He went about the villages in a circuit, teaching. (Mark 6:5–6)

Unbelief shut out the people of Nazareth from experiencing the manifestation of God's miracle power flowing through

Jesus. He was ready to heal and set free all who were oppressed and bound by infirmity. But unbelief had taken hold in the hearts of the people. The Word says that Jesus *"marveled"*—He was shocked and surprised—by their unbelief.

The eager faith of people in other towns is in distinct contrast to this. In Gennesaret, the people sent word throughout the region and brought to Jesus all who were diseased, *"and begged Him that they might only touch the hem of His garment. And as many as touched it were made perfectly well."* (Matthew 14:36). Near Galilee, great multitudes came to Jesus bringing the blind, lame, and mute, and He healed them. (See Matthew 15:30.) In Syria, they brought to Him the demon-possessed and people with all types of sicknesses, diseases, and infirmities, and He healed them. (See Matthew 4:23–24.) A great multitude came from throughout Judea and Jerusalem, and from Tyre and Sidon, to be healed of their diseases, and Jesus *"healed them all."* (See Luke 6:17–19.) In Capernaum, they brought people with all types of sicknesses and diseases, and Jesus *"laid His hands on every one of them and healed them"* (Luke 4:40).

> The church has not experienced God's miracle power on a greater scale because we have limited Him through a lack of faith.

What made the difference between the mighty manifestations of miracles that took place among the people from Gennesaret, Galilee, Syria, Judea, Jerusalem, Tyre, Sidon, and Capernaum and what happened in Nazareth? Again, a stronghold of unbelief hindered the release of the miraculous. As we noted earlier, a stronghold is any place where Satan takes up residence and exalts himself above the will, plans, and purposes of God. It is a powerful grip of the enemy. Satan has established strongholds over individuals, families, cities, and nations—strongholds of greed, promiscuousness, deception, hatred, and many other evils. He has gained strongholds in people's lives through their mind-sets—strongholds of intimidation, low self-esteem, pride, and fear.

Is there a struggle going on within you to believe for your miracle?

There is such a struggle going on within the hearts of many Christians. They believe in the awesome miracles God performed for Israel. They believe in the miracles that were manifested through Christ. Yet they struggle to believe that God will work a miracle on their behalf or that God will manifest His miracle power through them on behalf of others.

Many people who need miracles in their lives are thinking, *I know miracles are possible. I know God has promised to supply all my needs, to heal my body, to deliver me in the circumstances I am facing, but will He do it for me?*

There was a man in the Bible who had this same struggle. His son was demon-possessed, and the demon caused the boy to convulse, foam at the mouth, and grind his teeth. The man brought his demon-possessed son to Jesus to be healed, and he wanted to believe, but there was still unbelief in his heart. Jesus was away at the time, so the man asked some of Jesus' disciples to heal the boy. But they could not cast out the demon and set the boy free from his torment. Some religious leaders were there, and they began to argue with the disciples about the matter. When Jesus arrived on the scene, He asked the scribes, *"What are you arguing with them about?"* (Mark 9:16 NIV).

The man who had brought his son to be healed explained that the disciples were unable to cure his son. Jesus rebuked the people's unbelief, saying, *"O faithless generation, how long shall I be with you? How long shall I bear with you? Bring him to Me"* (Mark 9:19).

The reason the boy had not been healed is clear. It was because of their faithlessness or unbelief.

Jesus asked the father, *"How long has this been happening to him?"* (Mark 9:21). The father replied, *"From childhood. And often he has thrown him both into the fire and into the water to destroy him. But if You can do anything, have compassion on us and help us"* (Mark 9:21–22).

The poor man was desperate. His son was possessed by an unclean spirit that had taken control over him. This spirit had tried to destroy him by casting him into fire and into water. It would throw him into such violent convulsions that it would almost pull him to pieces. The boy was in such torment; he was wasting away before his father's eyes, and there was nothing the father could do—in the natural.

The man's first attempt in asking for healing had failed. Now here he was at the feet of Jesus, crying out for His mercy and compassion to heal his son.

Yet note that the man questioned Jesus' power to heal. He said, *"If You can do anything, have mercy on us."* (See verse 22.)

IF! The question is not *if* Christ is willing to work a miracle in your life or *if* He has power to heal, save, deliver, or meet whatever other need you may have. The question is whether or not you will tear down the stronghold of unbelief and have faith that He will do what He has promised. Jesus came to save, heal, deliver, and set people free from all the power of Satan. (See 1 John 3:8.) There is no question about whether He is able or willing to heal.

The healing of this demon-possessed boy was therefore dependent upon one thing—the father's ability to believe. Jesus placed the responsibility upon him, saying, *"If you can believe, all things are possible to him who believes"* (Mark 9:23).

> **To walk in the miraculous, we must move beyond unbelief to faith that transcends our circumstances.**

He was saying, "If you can believe, all things are possible. If you can believe, your son will be healed."

Tears welled up in the man's eyes as he cried out from the depths of his spirit, *"Lord, I believe; help my unbelief!"* (Mark 9:24). In that moment, as he stood there before Christ, he received and believed the words that Jesus spoke. Jesus had said, *"All things are possible"* (v. 23). That included the healing of his boy. His son could be set free, once and for all, from the terrible torment and affliction he had been suffering for so long.

The man believed the words Christ spoke to him, but he added, *"Help my unbelief"* (v. 24). He knew he needed Christ to help him overcome the unbelief still in his heart, and we need the same thing. Jesus had compassion on the man and his son, and He healed the boy.

BREAKING THROUGH TO THE SUPERNATURAL

This account clearly illustrates that unbelief will hinder the miracle flow of God in our lives. However, it will never stop God from manifesting His miracle power on the earth. Never! *"For what if some did not believe? Will their unbelief make the faithfulness of God without effect? Certainly not! Indeed, let God be true but every man a liar"* (Romans 3:3–4).

To walk in the miraculous, we must move beyond unbelief to faith that transcends our limited human mind-set and our seemingly overpowering circumstances. Unless you come to God in simple, childlike faith, believing that He will do exactly what He has promised, you will never be able to break through into the supernatural. The author of the book of Hebrews wrote, *"But without faith it is impossible to please Him, for he who comes to God must believe that He is, and that He is a rewarder of those who diligently seek Him"* (Hebrews 11:6).

When you come before the Lord, you must believe He is a *"rewarder"*—that He will reward your faith and release His miracle power to meet your need. You must come to Him without doubt. James said, *"But let him ask in faith, nothing wavering. For he that wavereth is like a wave of the sea driven with the wind and tossed. For let not that man think that he shall receive any thing of the Lord"* (James 1:6–7 KJV).

When you waver, your faith is up one day and down the next, depending on how you feel, what your circumstances are, and the type of sickness, financial crisis, or other problem you are facing. Yet Jesus said,

For assuredly, I say to you, whoever says to this mountain, "Be removed and be cast into the sea," and does not doubt in his heart, but believes that those things he says will be done, he will have whatever he says. Therefore I say to you, whatever things you ask when you pray, believe that you receive them, and you will have them. (Mark 11:23–24)

It is time for Christians to stop being double-minded. Either we believe God is a miracle-working God and that He will do all He has promised to do, or we believe He is a liar.

I choose to believe He is the almighty God of miracles, the God of the impossible, whose Word never fails and who still releases His miracle power on behalf of those who believe and trust Him.

What about you?

In one of my revival meetings in Illinois, a young man who had been completely deaf in one ear since birth requested prayer. He had never heard a sound in that ear. We prayed for him and laid hands on him (see Mark 16:18), and the healing virtue of Christ flowed into his body.

In a moment of time, he could hear even a whisper in that ear.

During that same revival, we prayed for a woman who had cancers on her face. As I prayed, I felt impressed to tell her that within three days the dreadful growths would fall from her face. Just as the Lord revealed to me, on the third day the cancers began to shrivel, dry up, and drop from her face!

In meetings across America and in other countries, I have witnessed sight restored to the blind, speech to the mute, and hearing to the deaf. I have seen people delivered from arthritis, tuberculosis, diabetes, ulcers, and many other kinds of problems. I could relate incident after incident in which God has wonderfully and miraculously delivered people from their afflictions.

Without a doubt, God has proven time and again that He still works miracles on behalf of those who come to Him in faith. He is the same mighty God. He has not changed. His miracle power is still the same, and He will release that power to meet whatever need you may have.

Reach out by faith right now and receive your miracle!

BRING YOUR EMOTIONS UNDER THE CONTROL OF THE HOLY SPIRIT

Many Christians are hindered from walking in the supernatural because they allow their emotions to control them. They are motivated and guided chiefly by their feelings. If they feel good, they have smiles on their faces and are ready to praise the Lord. But when illness or financial problems come and they feel pain or are discouraged, they begin to doubt their Christian experience or wonder why they don't have enough faith to receive a miracle from God.

You cannot live by your emotions. Regardless of how you may feel or what the physical evidence declares, you must continue to speak God's language—faith. You must not be tied to or dependent upon the way you feel when you face Satan's attacks on your body, home, or finances. God wants to bring you into a new dimension of strength whereby, regardless of how you may *feel*, you will be able to speak forth the Word of God into your circumstances and your need will be met.

Analyze your own personal environment. Are you allowing your feelings to hinder you from releasing your faith?

Concentrate on the circumstances you are facing right now. Are you suffering from an illness or disease that has plagued you for years? Perhaps you find yourself alone—your husband has left you and the children and now he wants a divorce. Or maybe you have just suffered a financial setback. You have lost your job and you don't know where your next meal is coming from.

Are you tired of resisting Satan's attacks on your body, home, or finances? Do you feel like giving up? Do you feel sad, discouraged, alone, or afraid? These are natural human emotions. If you look closely at the lives of all the great men and women of God throughout the Bible—such as Abraham, Sarah, David, Elijah, Esther, Peter, and Paul—you will see that they experienced discouragement, feelings of rejection, and fear. Sometimes these emotions influenced or threatened to influence their actions.

> **When you *know* that God is in control, you will be able to resist the temptation to give in to your feelings.**

In Mark 5:25–34, we read about the woman with the issue of blood, who had suffered for twelve long years and spent all her money on doctors trying to find a cure. Even after all her suffering, she did not allow her feelings to control her. She broke out of the natural world and her personal environment—her physical ailment and the mental turmoil she had experienced—and entered into the supernatural, where her faith took control and she received her miracle from Jesus.

The key to taking authority and dominion over your emotions is to have the same deep, inner knowing that Paul expressed when he faced adverse circumstances:

> *We are pursued (persecuted and hard driven), but not deserted [to stand alone]; we are struck down to the ground, but never struck out and destroyed....Therefore we do not become discouraged (utterly spiritless, exhausted, and wearied out through fear). Though our outer man is [progressively] decaying and wasting away, yet our inner self is being [progressively] renewed day after day.*
>
> (2 Corinthians 4:9, 16 AMP)

When you know, beyond all doubt, that God is in control, regardless of the circumstances you face, you will be able to resist the temptation to give in to your feelings and will be able to submit them to the control of the Holy Spirit.

TAKE DOMINION AND AUTHORITY OVER THE WORDS YOU SPEAK

Finally, but very importantly, analyze the words you speak. What are you saying concerning the circumstance in your life that needs a supernatural manifestation of God's power?

Are they words spoken in faith?

Are they words controlled by the Holy Spirit?

You can break through your personal environment into the miraculous as you begin to take control over your words and release the powerful Word of God into your circumstances. The Word in your mouth is full of the power of God. The Lord said,

So shall My word be that goes forth from My mouth; it shall not return to Me void, but it shall accomplish what I please, and it shall prosper in the thing for which I sent it.

(Isaiah 55:11)

God is not a man, that He should lie, nor a son of man, that He should repent. Has He said, and will He not do? Or has He spoken, and will He not make it good?

(Numbers 23:19)

Refuse to speak words of unbelief, fear, discouragement, or defeat. When you continually talk about your difficulties and negative circumstances—sickness, financial problems, marriage problems—and speak words of unbelief and fear, you block the manifestation of God's miracle power in your life.

The same miracle power that was released through Christ as He spoke life, healing, and deliverance two thousand years ago is in His Word. He said, *"The words that I speak to you are spirit, and they are life"* (John 6:63).

As you begin to speak words of faith, power, and victory, and as you confess God's promises, you will feel His Spirit within you quickening—releasing a flow of His power into your life. Without waiting for a visible change in your circumstances or an outward manifestation of the miracle you need, begin to praise God for it. Paul told the believers in Rome, *"'The word is near you, in your mouth and in your heart' (that is, the word of faith which we preach)"* (Romans 10:8).

Are there circumstances in your life requiring a miracle? Break through your personal environment. The moment you open your mouth to pray and declare God's promise into your situation, *believe* that you have received it. Jesus said, *"Therefore I say to you, whatever things you ask when you pray, believe that you receive them, and you will have them"* (Mark 11:24).

The power for the manifestation of the miracle is not in man or in anything he possesses. The power is in the Word.

The Word of God in your mouth is alive! It is the seed for your miracle. God's Word cannot fail. When you line up your life with His Word and speak forth His promises, you are talking God's language. To walk in the supernatural, your conversation must be filled with His Word, and you must act in accordance with it.

> **The power for the manifestation of your miracle is in the Word of God.**

As you speak forth God's Word into your circumstances, by faith, and act upon what He has promised, you will overcome natural limitations and take hold of the supernatural power of God.

A SUPERNATURAL ENVIRONMENT OF MIRACLES

As you break through the natural limitations of your personal environment, you will start living in an atmosphere whereby you can experience miracles in every area of your life. When you are walking in the supernatural, what you think about and meditate on is influenced and governed by the Holy Spirit and faith that is based on the Word of God. I encourage you to…

- break through from being governed and controlled by your carnal mind—with its will, thoughts, and imaginations—to having the mind of Christ whereby your will, thoughts, and imaginations can be influenced and controlled by the Holy Spirit.

- break through from relying on your own limited natural wisdom, understanding, and abilities to reaching out in faith to rely on the unlimited, supernatural power of God manifested in and through you.

- break through the limitation of your emotions by speaking the Word of God as the seed for your miracle.

- break through *every* natural limitation and take hold of the supernatural power of God to do the impossible!

Remember and apply these major keys to breaking through your natural environment:

1. Live according to the mind of Christ.

2. Take every thought captive to the obedience of Christ.

3. Tear down the stronghold of unbelief.

4. Bring your emotions under the control of the Holy Spirit.

5. Take dominion and authority over the words you speak.

PERSONAL APPLICATION

We have seen in this chapter that one of the biggest hindrances you will face in walking in the supernatural is your own personal living environment.

Through the power of the Holy Spirit, bring every thought into captivity to the obedience of Christ. (See 2 Corinthians 10:4–5.) Though doubt and unbelief are major strongholds that must be torn down before we can walk in the supernatural, there are other hindrances, such as spiritual ignorance, a mind-set that is based upon wrong information, the negative influence of others, and fear. You must learn to recognize any and all strongholds and tear them down in Jesus' name.

Remember, the power for the fulfillment of God's Word is not in you or in anything you possess. The power for the manifestation of your miracle is in the *Word*. Fill your mind with God's promises and continue to speak them into your circumstances.

God's Word in your mouth is life. Speak God's Word In faith, and act upon what He has promised!

CHAPTER SIX

DEVELOPING SUPERNATURAL EYESIGHT

Another strategic means of breaking through your natural environment is to develop supernatural vision. As long as you keep your eyes on the circumstances, problems, needs, and impossibilities you face, you will not be in a position to receive God's miraculous provision, and things may never change. In fact, things may even grow worse. When you have supernatural eyesight, however, you can take hold of God's promises as a present reality, even though you may not see or perceive them with your natural senses.

When you face a tremendous challenge or heartbreaking circumstance, such as tragedy, sickness, a financial crisis, or an impossible situation that cannot be met by natural means, do you keep your eyes on your circumstances instead of on our supernatural God?

Focusing on your circumstances will hinder you from seeing Him as He really is: the almighty God who stands ready to release His power on your behalf and to meet you with a miracle at your point of need. When you take your eyes off your circumstances and begin to view them not as problems, but as *miracle opportunities*, you will break through the limitations of your natural mind. Faith will rise up within you, and you will take a step into the supernatural.

SEEING CIRCUMSTANCES AS MIRACLE OPPORTUNITIES

To better understand how to do this, let's trace the steps of a man who had supernatural eyesight and knew what it meant to walk in God's miraculous power: the apostle Paul.

> **Real victory comes *during* your trial, sickness, or pain— not after it.**

Have you ever desired to be like Paul, having the same anointing that was upon his life? We gain an idea of the degree to which God's supernatural power flowed through him when we read that *"even handkerchiefs or aprons were brought from his body to the sick, and the diseases left them and the evil spirits went out of them"* (Acts 19:12).

Let's review a few of the miracles Paul was involved in. In Lystra, the power of God flowed through him to heal a man crippled from birth. (See Acts 14:8.) In Philippi, he cast a spirit of divination out of a slave girl. (See Acts 16:18.) In Troas, he raised Eutychus from the dead. (See Acts 20:9–12.)

Yet two instances especially stand out to me as revealing the supernatural power and strength in which Paul walked. The first occurred right after he had cast out the spirit of divination from the slave girl. His circumstances, in the natural, became very negative. (See Acts 16:19–24.) He and his partner Silas were…

- falsely accused.
- beaten after having their clothes stripped off.
- cast into prison, and their feet were placed in stocks.

If ever Paul needed a divine intervention from God, this was the time!

Imagine being in his place. How would you have reacted? What would have been your attitude under those conditions? Most Christians today would not have known how to cope. They would have been fearful, confused, angry, outraged, and full of self-pity. Many would have questioned God, saying, "Why have You allowed this to happen to me? Don't You love me?"

Again, some Christians feel that victory is the absence of pain or problems in their lives. Or they believe that victory comes only when a battle is over—when their pain is gone or when their financial problems are solved.

God didn't promise us we would never know sickness, pain, or sorrow. It is not His will to take away all our problems and adverse circumstances, but for us to receive the manifestation and fulfillment of His will and Word. Jesus said, *"These things I have spoken to you, that in Me you may have peace. In the world you will have tribulation; but be of good cheer, I have overcome the world"* (John 16:33).

Real victory comes *during* your trial, sickness, or pain—not after it.

Think about Paul in prison. He was seated on the hard, cold ground, unable to move, his feet fastened securely in the stocks. Blood was pouring from the wounds on his back. Yet in the middle of these circumstances, he had a deep inner knowing that God was in control of his circumstances and that He would deliver him. (See Acts 16:25–40.)

I can almost see Paul slowly raise his eyes and hands toward heaven. In the midst of his circumstances, songs of praise and worship begin to flow out of his mouth to God. Louder and louder, his voice echoes throughout and beyond the cell. Silas joins in, and their voices fill the night air until God's powerful presence permeates the entire prison.

Suddenly, God supernaturally intervenes in their circumstances with a miracle. He sends an earthquake that shakes the very foundations of the prison. All the prison doors are opened and everyone's chains are loosed.

God not only intervened in Paul and Silas' circumstances and met their need with a miracle, but, as a result of the manifestation of God's power, the jailer also came running to them asking what he must do to be saved!

The next incident is when Paul was a prisoner on a ship headed for Rome, ready to give a defense of the gospel to Caesar. (See Acts 27:14–28:10.) The ship on which he was sailing was beset by a storm and everyone on board had given up hope that they would be saved.

Once again, God supernaturally intervened in Paul's circumstances. He sent an angel to reassure Paul that He would deliver him and everyone else on the ship. Note Paul's complete confidence as he told the others, in the middle of this raging storm,

> *There stood by me this night an angel of the God to whom I belong and whom I serve, saying, "Do not be afraid, Paul;*

you must be brought before Caesar; and indeed God has granted you all those who sail with you." Therefore take heart, men, for I believe God that it will be just as it was told me. (Acts 27:23–25)

The soldiers who were guarding Paul and the other prisoners had planned to kill them, fearing their escape, but God protected Paul and the others. The ship was destroyed, but, just as the angel had said, everyone on board survived. They wrecked on the island of Mclita, and came ashore. While Paul was helping to gather firewood, he was bitten by a poisonous snake.

Once more, God supernaturally intervened to spare his life. Paul simply shook the snake off and went about his business.

The miracle power of God continued to flow through him. He prayed for Publius, the father of the chief official of the island, and he was healed. He also laid hands on many others on the island who had diseases, and they were healed.

> **Where there is a continual flow of God's life and a faith that overcomes, each trial and test will be met by His power.**

There are many other examples from the lives of Paul, Jesus' disciples, and a number of others in the Bible that illustrate how God's miracle power can flow through those who believe in Him. The circumstances they faced were opportunities for God's supernatural power to be released. The same is true in your life. You do not have to be a spiritual giant like the apostle Paul to walk in the supernatural knowing that God will intervene in your circumstances and work a miracle on your behalf. Your circumstances are opportunities for God's power to be released.

EACH TRIAL AND TEST WILL BE MET BY GOD'S POWER

We should understand that walking in the supernatural involves down-to-earth, day-to-day living. Problems will come. Trials and testing will come. But where there is a continual flow of God's life being manifested in and through our lives, and where there is a faith that overcomes, each trial and test will be met by His power.

- You may be struggling under a heavy financial burden.
- You may be battling a debilitating or terminal disease.
- Your husband or wife may have left you and may be suing for divorce.
- Your loved one may be bound by drugs or alcohol.

Whatever circumstance you face, refuse to allow your mind to remain focused on the natural situation or your natural limitations. Regardless of how you feel, or what you think or see, set your focus on God and His unlimited supernatural power.

Let me relate a miracle of healing I experienced in my ministry that was as real as the great miracles manifested in the New Testament. I was in Honduras for a citywide campaign. We had rented the city auditorium, which seated several thousand people. On the very first night, after I had preached a brief message on faith, I felt the Holy Spirit said to me, "Minister to the sick."

I immediately called for all the people in the congregation who wanted to receive prayer for healing to come and stand in the prayer line. While men and women began lining up all the way around the huge auditorium, the Holy Spirit again spoke to me, saying, "God is going to heal the first five people in the prayer line tonight."

As I started praying for the sick, I asked the first man standing in line what was the nature of his need. A man standing near him answered, "This man is totally deaf and mute."

I asked the second man and again was informed that he was deaf and mute.

The third man had the same affliction, as well as the fourth and fifth.

> **Satan cannot bring any circumstances into your life that can separate you from God's love.**

When I learned this, it was as if the devil jumped on my shoulder, as he had done in the earlier incident I mentioned, and said, "You've really played the fool now. If your God does not heal these people, you are going to have to pack your bags and go home."

I wasn't intimidated by him one bit. I responded with great confidence, "Yes, devil. But when God does heal them, you're going to look like a fool, and you're going to have to pack your bags and get out of town. God has already told me He is going to heal the first five people in this line, and if God says it, He will do it. You can depend on God doing what He promises!"

I laid my hand on the first man and spoke directly to the deaf and mute spirit, "You foul, deaf and dumb spirit, you know who I am. I'm T. L. Lowery, a servant of the Most High God. You know that God has given me power and authority over your power in Jesus' name, and I command you to come out of this man and be assigned to the pit of hell, bound in chains of everlasting darkness until the day of judgment."

The moment I prayed that prayer, I felt the Holy Spirit surge through my body, and I knew that God had performed a miracle. The man had fallen to the floor, so I leaned over to him and said softly, "Say 'Hallelujah.'"

When I said that, the man flinched because he heard for the first time in his life. A smile came across his face, and he said, "Hallelujah!" He was not mumbling or mouthing something unintelligible. He said it clearly and distinctly.

I turned to the second man. Before I could address him, *he* grinned and shouted, "Hallelujah!" The third man shouted, "Hallelujah!" The fourth shouted, "Hallelujah!" The fifth shouted, "Hallelujah!" God had healed every one of the five men *simultaneously*. I rejoiced in the power of God's deliverance and joined them in shouting, "Hallelujah!"

You must realize there are two forces ready to work in the midst of your circumstances: (1) God stands ready to meet you at the point of your need and release His miracle power; (2) Satan stands ready to use your circumstances to defeat you and to accuse God.

The circumstances that come into your life are not by chance. If you have been born again and are walking in obedience to God, you are considered righteous in His eyes, and the Word of God says that your steps are *"ordered by the LORD"* (Psalm 37:23). This idea may be hard for you to understand, especially if you have recently experienced tragedy and heartache in your life. Yet once you realize there are two forces at work in the circumstances of your life, and learn how to see beyond your situations and determine who you will allow to be in control of those circumstances, you will not be fearful.

The Bible is clear. God is totally good. There is no evil in Him. He does not tempt man. (See James 1:13.) He does not send problems. He does not send financial disasters. He does not cause marriages to break up. He does not send pain or sickness. He does not bring death and destruction. God cannot act contrary to His Word. He sent His only Son into the world to *destroy the works of the devil* (1 John 3:8), so we might have life more abundantly. (See John 10:10.) It is through Jesus Christ that you can take hold of God's promises by faith and receive miracle provisions.

There may be times when God will allow certain circumstances to come into your life to build and test your faith and bring you into a new level of spiritual maturity. But He will never allow any circumstance to come into your life that is greater than you are able to bear. (See 1 Corinthians 10:13.) When you face situations that seem unbearable or impossible, the Lord will not leave you, but will, during the battle, provide a solution…a great victory…a miracle.

Always remember that Satan cannot bring any circumstances into your life that can separate you from God or His love. (See Romans 8:35–37.) Using his power of deception, Satan will come to you at the point of your need and try to fill your heart with fear. He will tell you that he is in control of your circumstances and that you are defeated. He will try to use the situations in your life to cause you to doubt God's promises and to accuse Him. He knows if he can keep your eyes on the problem and block you from seeing the solution God has for you, the circumstances will appear too big for you.

One day Jesus passed a man who was blind from birth. His disciples asked him, *"Rabbi, who sinned, this man or his parents, that he was born blind?"* (John 9:2 NIV). Notice Christ's answer: *"Neither this man nor his parents sinned,…but this happened so that the work of God might be displayed in his life"* (v. 3 NIV).

People looked upon this man as a hopeless, blind beggar. In the natural, his circumstances were impossible. But, when Jesus looked at him, He saw a *miracle opportunity* for the power of God to be manifested in this man's life. Jesus spit on the ground, made some mud of the spittle, and put it on the blind man's eyes. He then told him to wash in the pool of Siloam. As the blind man obeyed, he was healed.

Whatever circumstances you face, therefore, refuse to allow Satan to intimidate you. Take your eyes off those circumstances and consider them *miracle opportunities* for God to manifest His power on your behalf.

IT IS WELL!

There was a Shunammite woman who exercised incredible faith and supernatural eyesight at her greatest time of need. (See 2 Kings 4:8–37.)

Her desperate situation involved her young son. His birth had been a miracle—a blessing from Jehovah, the God of the prophet Elisha. Yet now, according to the circumstances, it looked as if death had taken him away from her.

DEVELOPING SUPERNATURAL EYESIGHT

How well she remembered that day when the prophet first told her she and her husband would have a child. Elisha had called her to the room she and her husband had made available for him on the roof of their house. As she stood in the doorway, Elisha had prophesied, in effect, "About this time next year, you will hold a son in your arms." At first she hadn't believed her ears. How could this be possible? Her husband was old and beyond the age of fathering a child. Was Elisha, the man of God, lying or trying to deceive her? She had responded, *"'No, my lord....Don't mislead your servant!'"* (2 Kings 4:16 NIV). But the miracle happened. She conceived, and just as Elisha had prophesied, the very next year she was holding her own son in her arms.

> **Refuse to keep your eyes on the natural. Instead, focus on our miracle-working God.**

I imagine that watching their son grow had given the woman and her husband great joy. Yet, one day, when the child went out to his father, who was with the reapers, the boy became physically distressed, saying, *"My head! My head!"* (2 Kings 4:19 NIV).

The father told a servant to take his son to his mother. The woman cradled him in her lap. How long she sat there, we do not know. But at noon her miracle child *died*.

This mother could have despaired, yet she did not react according to the natural circumstances she faced. She did not begin to cry or weep hysterically. She did not blame God or question why this had happened. She did not scream for someone to come help her. She didn't even call for her husband. Instead, she carried the lifeless body of her son up to Elisha's room, laid him on the bed, shut the door, and went out.

To the natural eye, nothing could be done for the boy. Yet this woman's eyes were not focused on the fact that her son was dead. She called for her husband and said, *"Please send me one of the servants and a donkey so I can go to the man of God quickly and return"* (2 Kings 4:22 NIV). When her husband questioned why she was going to see the prophet that day, she didn't tell him their son was dead. She said, *"It's all right"* (v. 23 NIV). Her heart and mind were not focused on the natural. She had experienced the miracle birth of her son, and her eyes were focused on a miracle-working God.

When she drew near to where Elisha was staying on Mt. Carmel, the prophet saw her in the distance and sensed something must be wrong. He said to his servant, Gehazi, in effect, "Look, there's the Shunammite woman! Go out to meet her. Ask her for me if everything is all right with her, her husband, and their child."

Notice again the woman's response. She did not tell Elisha's servant that her son was dead. Instead, she told Gehazi, *"It is well"* (2 Kings 4:26). Her eyes were not on her circumstances. She left her son's lifeless body at home and went directly to the prophet because she believed the same God of Elisha who had given her a son could also bring him back from the dead. Otherwise, she would have stayed at home and called for the mourners.

When the Shunammite woman reached Elisha, she fell on the ground and grabbed hold of his feet. Gehazi came to push her away, yet Elisha told him to leave her alone. He could see she was deeply troubled, but God had not revealed her problem to him. The woman asked in distress, *"Did I ask you for a son, my lord?...Didn't I tell you, 'Don't raise my hopes'?"* (2 Kings 4:28 NIV).

From her heart-wrenching pleas, Elisha knew the woman's boy was dead. He told Gehazi to run to her house and *"lay [his] staff on the boy's face"* (2 Kings 4:29 NIV). But the dead child's mother still did not give up. She told Elisha, *"As surely as the LORD lives and as you live, I will not leave you"* (2 Kings 4:30 NIV). In other words, she was telling Elisha that she was not going to leave him until he went personally to pray for her boy. Her eyes were focused on a miracle. Only the word of faith and the prayer of the man of God could help her son.

Seeing the woman's strong, determined perseverance, Elisha got up and started back with her. In the meantime, Gehazi had gone ahead and placed Elisha's staff on the boy's face, but nothing had happened. He went back to meet Elisha and told him, *"The boy has not awakened"* (2 Kings 4:31 NIV).

We don't know how much time had elapsed since the boy had died in his mother's arms. But, no doubt, it had been many hours. The first attempt to raise her son from the dead had failed. Elisha and the Shunammite woman returned to her house only to find out the boy was indeed still dead.

At that point, the woman had every natural reason to give up, but she didn't. Her eyes remained focused on the miracle she needed for her son. She didn't see him as dead, but alive.

Elisha went into the room, shut the door, and began to pray. Then he twice stretched himself out on the boy's lifeless body. As the supernatural power of God began to flow through Elisha to the boy, the life of God raised him up.

This woman received her son back from the dead because she refused to keep her eyes focused on the natural and instead focused on the miracle-working God of Elisha.

FROM NATURAL TO SUPERNATURAL EYESIGHT

To walk in the supernatural, you must learn not to live your life according to what you see with your natural eyes or perceive with your natural understanding. If the Shunammite woman had gone by what she saw with her natural eyes, her son would never have been resurrected from the dead. Likewise, if you want to live in this new spiritual dimension God is bringing the church into, you must move from natural to *supernatural* vision.

> *For we walk by faith [we regulate our lives and conduct ourselves by our conviction or belief respecting man's relationship to God and divine things, with trust and holy fervor; thus we walk] not by sight or appearance.*
>
> (2 Corinthians 5:7 AMP)

The only way you will dare to be lifted to a higher spiritual plateau than you have ever experienced is to have a spiritual breakthrough where you are no longer living according to what you see with your natural eyesight. God must open your eyes so that you will begin to see beyond the limitations of the natural into the supernatural realm of the Holy Spirit.

Put yourself in the shoes of the Shunammite woman. What would you have done? How would you have reacted?

DEVELOPING SUPERNATURAL EYESIGHT

The reason why so many Christians are living below what God intended for them to experience as His sons and daughters is that they see only with their natural eyesight, and they react according to their five natural senses. When faced with sickness, financial crisis, or family problems, they depend upon themselves and their natural resources as they cry out, "What are *we* going to do?" instead of looking to our supernatural God for a miracle.

This was the reaction of Elisha's servant, Gehazi, during another incident, when he saw the great army that the king of Syria had sent to capture or kill them. (See 2 Kings 6:8–17.) The entire city where they were staying was surrounded by Syrian horses and chariots. Gehazi had already observed the supernatural power of God and how Elisha had raised the Shunammite woman's son from the dead. Yet he was still governed by his natural vision and

> **A spirit of fear will block you from receiving the miracle you need.**

reacted to their circumstances according to what he saw. He ran to Elisha and said, *"Oh, my Lord, what shall we do?"* (2 Kings 6:15 NIV). Have you ever looked at your circumstances or problems and said, "I just don't know what we are going to do"?

Elisha was a man with tremendous supernatural eyesight. When he looked at the great Syrian army surrounding him and the city, he did not become fearful or run and hide. He was not worried. He saw something the natural eye could not see. While Gehazi saw the city surrounded by the Syrian army, with its vast multitude of earthly soldiers, chariots, and horses, Elisha saw the mountain covered with God's horses and chariots of fire! He told Gehazi, *"Don't be afraid....Those who are with us are more than those who are with them"* (2 Kings 6:16 NIV).

If you continue to focus your eyes on the natural realm—on your emotional pain, the doctor's report, your financial problems, or the seeming impossibility of your circumstances, you will open the door to fear and doubt, as did Gehazi. These things will be barriers to your receiving the fulfillment of God's promises.

For example, a spirit of fear may grab hold of you so that you begin thinking your condition is going to grow worse, that nothing can be done, and that you might as well give up hope. Your faith will begin to waver, and you will begin to question God and His Word, asking,

- "Why hasn't God healed me?"
- "Why hasn't God saved my children?"
- "Why doesn't God answer my prayers?"

A spirit of fear will block you from receiving the miracle you need. If you allow it to remain, it will paralyze your faith and cause unbelief to gain a stronghold. And it will be sin because *"whatever is not from faith is sin"* (Romans 14:23).

Jesus said it is those who do not doubt in their hearts who will receive whatever they ask. (See Mark 11:23.) Those who come to God must come in faith *without wavering*. People who have fear and doubt in their hearts will waver, and they will not receive anything from the Lord. (See James 1:6–7.) Again, to walk daily in the supernatural, you must break through fear and doubt and begin to see every adverse circumstance, pain, heartache, disappointment, or financial adversity that comes into your life as a *miracle opportunity*.

It wasn't until Elisha prayed for Gehazi that God opened his eyes and he was able to see the great army of God, the horses and chariots of fire surrounding and protecting them from the enemy. The cry of my heart is that God will open your eyes so you will be able to see the supernatural provision He has provided for you in the circumstances you face.

Like Gehazi, our spiritual eyes must be opened by the Holy Spirit before we can see all God has provided for us and take hold of the miracles we need. We must have the scales removed from our eyes, as the apostle Paul did when he received both physical and spiritual vision at his conversion. (See Acts 9:1–20.) Jesus told the lukewarm, self-satisfied church of Laodicea, *"Anoint your eyes with eye salve, that you may see"* (Revelation 3:18). When we look with eyes that are anointed by the Spirit, we see beyond the natural into the fullness of God's power and glory.

QUALITIES OF SUPERNATURAL EYESIGHT

Supernatural eyesight is therefore the ability to see, perceive, and understand things that are beyond the natural realm. It enables us to see into the invisible realm of the Spirit, into the unlimited, immeasurable riches of God's power and glory, so we can take hold of miracles.

Throughout the ages, men and women who have walked closely with God and possessed supernatural eyesight have tapped into His power to transcend the laws of nature. We already saw the examples of the apostle Paul, Elijah, and the Shunammite woman. Let's look at some additional examples as we note the following qualities of supernatural eyesight.

NOT LIMITED BY TIME OR SPACE

Over one thousand years before Christ was born, Abraham exercised spiritual eyesight when he "saw" the day Christ, the promised Messiah, would come to redeem humanity from sin. Jesus said, *"Your father Abraham rejoiced to see My day, and he saw it and was glad"* (John 8:56).

PENETRATES THE INVISIBLE

Abraham also looked into the invisible, eternal realm to the city of the living God, the heavenly Jerusalem. *"For he looked for a city which hath foundations, whose builder and maker is God"* (Hebrews 11:10 KJV). He didn't give up hope, but kept his faith alive, vibrant, and focused. As a result, he took hold of the promises of God. *"And so, after he had patiently endured, he obtained the promise"* (Hebrews 6:15).

TRANSCENDS THE NATURAL REALM TO CAPTURE THE IMPOSSIBLE

Moses was able to do what was naturally impossible because he had supernatural eyesight and saw the all-powerful, invisible God. The writer of the book of Hebrews said, *"[Motivated] by faith he left Egypt behind him, being unawed and undismayed by the wrath of the king; for he never flinched but held staunchly to his purpose and endured steadfastly as one who **gazed on Him Who is invisible**"* (Hebrews 11:27 AMP, emphasis added).

After his encounter with God at the burning bush, Moses faced the pharaoh of Egypt and demanded that he let the children of Israel go. Because he saw into the supernatural realm—and focused his eyes on Jehovah God Almighty—he walked in the realm of the miraculous.

Moses not only *saw,* but he also *believed* God would do as He promised. As a result, the "impossible" happened. The Red Sea parted. Manna rained down from heaven for forty years. God led the Israelites with a pillar of cloud by day and a pillar of fire by night. And the people of Israel eventually went into the Promised Land.

Fifteen centuries later, a Roman centurion who had supernatural eyesight appealed to Jesus to heal his servant, who was lying at home *"grievously tormented"* with palsy. (See Matthew 8:5–13 KJV.) Palsy was a form of paralysis with contraction of the joints and was accompanied by intense suffering. The centurion was not even a part of the nation of Israel. He was a Gentile, a heathen. Yet despite the prejudice of the Romans toward the Jews, this centurion had developed a love for the people and nation of Israel and had built the synagogue at Capernaum. (See Luke 7:3–5.)

> **You are not the one doing the works of God; it is Christ, who is living His life through you.**

He had not grown up knowing about the mighty God of Israel and His supernatural power in delivering Israel out of Egyptian bondage. But he had heard about Jesus and His power to heal. When Jesus heard his request, His immediate response was, *"I will come and heal him"* (v. 7). He did not hesitate; He said, "I will." He was willing and ready to go to the centurion's house to heal his servant.

The Roman centurion broke through the limitations of his natural sight and recognized Jesus for who He was, saying, *"Lord, I am not worthy that You should come under my roof. But only speak a word, and my servant will be healed"* (Luke 7:8).

The centurion did not just see a man—a Galilean who had come down from the mountains with His friends to Capernaum. Neither did he see Jesus as just another prophet. His supernatural eyesight saw an unlimited, all-powerful Being. He saw One with absolute authority and dominion over all sickness, and over every other power.

In Christ's presence, the centurion recognized his own unworthiness and told Him it wasn't even necessary for Him to come to his house to heal his servant. Knowing who Christ was, with His unlimited power and authority, he said, *"But **only speak a word,** and my servant will be healed."*

There was no doubt or questioning in the centurion's mind as to whether Christ had the power to heal his servant or whether He was willing. He had a *revelation* of Christ and placed complete faith in His ability to heal.

Jesus was amazed at the centurion's statement and said to His disciples and the others following Him, *"Assuredly, I say to you, I have not found such great faith, not even in Israel!"* (Matthew 8:10). Then He said to the centurion, *"Go your way; and as you have believed, so let it be done for you"* (v. 13).

At that very moment—as Jesus spoke—God's divine healing power was released into the body of the servant, miles away, and he was healed. *"And his servant was healed that same hour"* (v. 13).

Jesus had been given power and authority over Satan and all powers and principalities. When He spoke, Satan and his demons had to go. When He spoke, every form of sickness and pain had to go.

The miracle power of God is unlimited!

- It transcends every natural limitation of time.
- It transcends the limitations of space.
- It goes beyond all natural limitations of human need.

As a child of God, you are a man or woman of power, authority, and dominion. You have been called, commissioned, anointed, and sent forth by Christ. You have not been sent forth to take authority over Satan in your own power. The works you do must be done according to what Christ has instructed and commanded you to do. You are not the one doing the works of God; it is Christ, the Living Word, who is living His life through you. When you rebuke Satan and his demons, they must obey. When you speak healing in the name of Jesus, sickness and pain must go.

Many Christians today place limitations on Christ because they see only through natural eyes. They may have inoperable cancer, a physical deformity, paralysis, or some longstanding illness that, according to the natural mind, is impossible. They cannot understand how they could ever be healed. Other Christians limit the miracle power of God because they are expecting Him to respond to their need according to their own preconceived ideas regarding the time, place, and method. When they do not receive their miracle or are not healed in the way they expect, they begin to waver, question, and doubt.

Yet when you have a revelation of Christ and see Him as He is—unlimited, all-powerful, unchanging—then, suddenly, what seems impossible becomes possible. Like the centurion, you must *see* Christ as He truly is and break through every limitation you have placed upon Him.

Just one glimpse of Christ and His unlimited power, and faith will be released within you to believe Him for the impossible.

You may face problems or have a specific urgent need in your life right now that has caused you to be fearful or worried. Regardless of whether your need is large or small, or whether your condition seems impossible to the natural mind, there is One who stands beside you and will bring His miracle power into your circumstances. This is the day for you to take your eyes off your desperate circumstances and put them on our miracle-working God. The Living Word is in you. He has written His Word on your heart. Let it come forth like a mighty, healing stream. Let the words come forth from your mouth, destroying the strongholds of the enemy. In the name of Jesus, break through every natural limitation.

> **When you have a revelation of Christ and see Him as He is, what seems impossible becomes possible.**

The things that seem hopeless and impossible with man are possible with God. Commanding the forces of nature so the sun and the weather obey the word of a man—impossible. Defying a law of physics to walk on water—impossible. But Joshua, Elijah, and Peter had supernatural vision. They possessed the ability not only to see beyond the limitations of what is considered impossible to human beings, but also *to do* the impossible.

The impossible occurred when Joshua commanded the sun to stop in the middle of the day so the Israelites could continue fighting and win a resounding victory over the Amorites:

> *Then Joshua spoke to the LORD in the day when the LORD delivered up the Amorites before the children of Israel, and he said in the sight of Israel: "Sun, stand still over Gibeon; and Moon, in the Valley of Aijalon." So the sun stood still, and the moon stopped, till the people had revenge upon their enemies. Is this not written in the Book of Jasher? So the sun stood still in the midst of heaven, and did not hasten to go down for about a whole day.* (Joshua 10:12–13)

The prophet Elijah's spiritual vision enabled him to command the forces of nature, also. He did the impossible when, by his word, he shut up the heavens for three-and-a-half years so that it did not rain. (See 1 Kings 17:1; James 5:17–18.) Then he spoke a word that opened the heavens and brought rain. He saw the rain cloud and the great outpouring of rain even before it appeared. He *heard* in his spirit the sound of the downpour of rain and told Ahab, the king, *"Go up, eat and drink; for there is the sound of abundance of rain"* (1 Kings 18:41). Elijah sent his servant back seven times to look for the rain clouds. He did not give up but persevered because he *saw* in his spirit and acted on the word God had spoken to him.

When his servant came back the seventh time and reported there was a small cloud, about the size of a man's hand, arising from the sea, Elijah told him, *"Go up, say to Ahab, 'Prepare your chariot, and go down before the rain stops you'"* (1 Kings 18:44).

In the meantime, the sky grew black with clouds. The wind began to roar, and a heavy rain began to fall. The Spirit of the Lord came upon Elijah, and he outran Ahab and his chariot all the way to Jezreel, which was a distance of about twenty miles!

Peter did the impossible when he walked on top of the waters of the Sea of Galilee. When Christ called out to Peter, *"Come"* (Matthew 14:29), Peter did not consider the fact that walking on water, in the natural, is impossible. He saw the unlimited power of Christ, and as long as his vision remained focused on Jesus, he broke through all natural limitations to walk on the water.

> **As long as Peter kept his focus on Jesus, he broke through natural limitations and walked on the water.**

It wasn't until he began to look with his natural eyes and to reason with his natural understanding that he began to sink in the water. When he focused his eyes on his physical circumstances, fear and doubt stopped the flow of the miraculous.

Smith Wigglesworth was a man with spiritual vision who walked in the supernatural. He ministered from the early 1900s to the 1940s and was called the Apostle of Faith because he believed and preached that God could do the impossible.

Through faith, Wigglesworth led tens of thousands around the world to Christ. Through faith, tens of thousands were healed under his hands and ministry: the deaf heard, the blind saw, the crippled walked, those with cancer were completely delivered and lived long lives. Through faith, he raised fourteen people from the dead, including his own wife, Polly, and saw multitudes raised up from their sickbeds.[16]

Wigglesworth depended fully on the Holy Spirit to flow through him. He lived in unbroken communion and fellowship with God and was continuously seeking God's presence. He said that he never went half an hour without praying, and he constantly prayed in tongues.[17] Wigglesworth described this miraculous event that occurred under his ministry:

> One day when I came home from our open-air meeting at eleven o'clock, I found that my wife was out. I asked, "Where is she?" I was told that she was down at Mitchell's. I had seen Mitchell that day and knew that he was at the point of death. I knew that it would be impossible for him to survive the day unless the Lord undertook to heal him....
>
> ...I hurried down to the house, and as I got near, I heard terrible screams. I knew that something had happened. I saw Mrs. Mitchell on the staircase and asked, "What's up?"
>
> She replied, "He is gone! He is gone!"
>
> I just passed by her and went into the room. Immediately I saw that Mitchell had gone. I could not understand it, but I began to pray. My wife was always afraid that I would go too far, and she laid hold of me

and said, "...Don't you see that he is dead?" I continued to pray and my wife continued to cry out to me... But I continued praying.

I got as far as I could with my own faith, and then God laid hold of me. Oh, it was such a laying hold that I could believe for anything. The faith of the Lord Jesus laid hold of me, and a solid peace came into my heart. I shouted, "He lives! He lives! He lives!" And he is living today.

There is a difference between our faith and the faith of the Lord Jesus. The faith of the Lord Jesus is needed. We must change faith from time to time. Your faith may get to a place where it wavers. The faith of Christ never wavers. When you have His faith, the thing is finished. When you have that faith, you will never look at things as they are. You will see the things of nature give way to the things of the Spirit; you will see the temporal swallowed up in the eternal.[18]

The following is an account of an awesome, creative miracle God manifested as a result of Smith Wigglesworth's ability to see and believe God for the impossible.

While staying in the home of a curate of the Church of England...[Wigglesworth] and the curate were sitting together talking after supper. No doubt the subject of their conversation was that the poor fellow had no legs. Artificial limbs in those days were unlike the sophisticated limbs of today.

Wigglesworth said to the man quite suddenly

(which he often did when ministering in cases like this), "Go and get a pair of new shoes in the morning."

The poor fellow thought it was some kind of joke. However, after Wigglesworth and the curate had retired to their respective rooms for the night, God said to the curate, "Do as My servant hath said." What a designation for any person—My servant! God was identifying Himself with Wigglesworth.

There was no more sleep for the man that night. He rose up early, went downtown, and stood waiting for the shoe shop to open. The manager eventually arrived and opened the shop for business. The curate went in and sat down.

Presently an assistant came and said, "Good morning, sir. Can I help you?"

The man said, "Yes, would you get me a pair of shoes, please?"

"Yes, sir. Size and color?"

The man hesitated. The assistant then saw his condition and said, "Sorry, sir. We can't help you."

"It is all right, young man. But I do want a pair of shoes. Size 8, color black."

The assistant went to get the requested shoes. A few minutes later he returned and handed them to the man. The man put one stump into a shoe, and instantly a foot and leg formed! Then the same thing happened with the other leg!

He walked out that shop, not only with a new pair of shoes, but also with a new pair of legs![19]

These are examples of the powerful supernatural dimension God intends the body of Christ to operate in to meet the desperate needs around us today, as living proof that He is the one true and living God.

FOCUS YOUR SPIRITUAL VISION

Remember that in the coming move of God, it will not be just the evangelists, ministers, and other well-known Christian leaders who are used in manifesting the supernatural power of God. All believers will be used in demonstrating His power as they step into the fulfillment of Christ's promise of doing *"greater works"* (John 14:12). With the supernatural eyesight the Father gives you, you will be able to see the greater works and then do them by the power of His Spirit within you.

> **Supernatural eyesight enables you to "see" God's greater works and then do them by the power of the Spirit.**

Your spiritual vision must not be limited by your circumstances, your need, your own abilities, your natural resources, or what you see with your natural eyes. The Father wants you to focus your spiritual vision so that you will see beyond the natural into the supernatural realm of the Spirit. Again, it is there that you will be able to take hold of His promises as a *present reality*, although you may not see or perceive them with your natural senses. Paul said, *"We do not look at the things which are seen, but at the things which are not seen. For the things which are seen are temporary, but the things which are not seen are eternal"* (2 Corinthians 4:18).

DEVELOPING SUPERNATURAL EYESIGHT

You must pray with your spiritual vision set and your faith firmly fixed upon your supernatural God, who has bound Himself to you with His Word. Then, believe and expect Him to release His power *into your circumstances.*

Paul prayed for the Ephesian believers, *"The eyes of your understanding being enlightened; that you may know what is the hope of His calling, what are the riches of the glory of His inheritance in the saints"* (Ephesians 1:18). The natural mind cannot fathom the depth and greatness of the Father's love and His provision for salvation, His awesome promises, the indwelling of the Holy Spirit, or His miracle-working power. The only way to have supernatural eyesight to see and perceive all the Father has provided for you is by the activation of faith within you.

> *Now faith is the assurance (the confirmation, the title deed) of the things [we] hope for, being the proof of things [we] do not see and the conviction of their reality [faith perceiving as real fact what is not revealed to the senses].*
>
> (Hebrews 11:1 AMP)

I like Andrew Murray's definition of faith: "It is the ear which has heard God say what He will do and the eye which has seen Him doing it."[20] Faith is the assurance—a firm persuasion—that God will do all He has promised. It is the evidence or proof of the things you are unable to see with your natural eyes. It reveals to your spirit the *reality* of the things you are believing God to do and enables you to take possession of them even *before* they are manifested to your natural senses.

As long as you keep your eyes focused on your problems instead of activating your faith to receive the miracle solution

God has for you, the circumstances you face will be too big for you. God wants you to develop your spiritual eyesight so that when you face obstacles or circumstances Satan has placed in your way to defeat you, you will not be discouraged but will be able to see, with your spiritual eyes, God supernaturally intervening on your behalf.

Don't wait until you see a physical manifestation with your natural eyes before you believe God for a miracle. Jesus said, *"Therefore I say to you, whatever things you ask when you pray, believe that you receive them, and you will have them"* (Mark 11:24). Focus your spiritual eyesight, activate your faith, and begin to see yourself healed…your marriage restored…God's provision being released in your finances—whatever need you face being met. Through eyes of faith, the Roman centurion *saw* his servant being healed at Christ's command *before* the healing was manifested.

> **Spiritual eyesight is developed through an intimate relationship with the Lord.**

Christ Himself lived and operated in a powerful supernatural dimension where His eyes were not focused on the circumstances and situations in the natural world, but on the invisible, eternal, almighty God, with whom nothing is impossible. He did absolutely nothing independent of the Father.

Jesus had "stripped" Himself of His divine abilities. (See Philippians 2:6–7.) Although He was the Son of God, He worked all His mighty miracles through the power of the Holy

Spirit. (See Acts 10:38.) Jesus said He worked His works—healing the sick, opening blind eyes, casting out demons, raising the dead—by first spiritually seeing the Father doing these works. *"The Son can do nothing of Himself, but what He sees the Father do; for whatever He does, the Son also does in like manner"* (John 5:19). Everything Jesus did was a result of what the Father revealed to Him while He waited in His presence in prayer, and by the Holy Spirit. *"The words that I speak to you I do not speak on My own authority; but the Father who dwells in Me does the works"* (John 14:10).

Likewise, the manifestation of God's miracle power and glory in your life will come as a result of your seeing in the Spirit realm what the Father is doing—and then doing what you see.

FOCUS YOUR SUPERNATURAL EYESIGHT

Supernatural eyesight is a by-product of the indwelling Holy Spirit working within you. It is not something you can manufacture. It is not something you can receive simply by someone imparting it to you through the laying on of hands. It is developed through an intimate relationship with the Lord—by spending time in His presence and seeking earnestly to know Him and hear His voice. It is developed as you fully surrender your life to the leading and direction of the Spirit.

God has given us a supernatural ability to hear and know His voice. Jesus said,

> *My sheep hear My voice, and I know them, and they follow Me.* (John 10:27)

But when He, the Spirit of Truth (the Truth-giving Spirit) comes, He will guide you into all the Truth (the whole, full Truth). For He will not speak His own message [on His own authority]; but He will tell whatever He hears [from the Father; He will give the message that has been given to Him], and He will announce and declare to you the things that are to come [that will happen in the future].

(John 16:13 AMP)

God wants you to develop supernatural eyesight to see things that will happen in the future before His return. He doesn't want you to be taken by surprise. He wants you to know and be prepared for His coming. We can know the plan and purposes of God and His will in all things.

The Holy Spirit knows everything, from the beginning to the end, about the earth, about our families, about our jobs. He will take us by the hand and lead us into the future, so that we can live in peace and assurance.

It is the work and ministry of the Holy Spirit in your life to reveal Christ in all His glory to you and to enable you to see and perceive the things God has prepared for you. Again, Paul wrote,

As it is written: "Eye has not seen, nor ear heard, nor have entered into the heart of man the things which God has prepared for those who love Him." But God has revealed them to us through His Spirit. For the Spirit searches all things, yes, the deep things of God. For what man knows the things of a man except the spirit of the man which is in him? Even so no one knows the things of God except the

DEVELOPING SUPERNATURAL EYESIGHT

Spirit of God. Now we have received, not the spirit of the world, but the Spirit who is from God, that we might know the things that have been freely given to us by God.

(1 Corinthians 2:9–12)

The Holy Spirit takes us step-by-step. He takes the things that are Christ's, that you and I long to know about, the secret things that are hidden, and reveals them to us.

Are you ready for God to remove the scales from your spiritual eyes so you will be able to see beyond the natural into the supernatural? What circumstances are you facing in which you need God to manifest His supernatural power? Do you need healing, a financial miracle, a miracle in your family, or a miracle in your ministry? Now that you have seen it is possible, do you long to walk in the supernatural with God's miracle power flowing in you and through you?

> **The Holy Spirit takes the hidden, secret things that are Christ's and reveals them to us.**

Focus your supernatural eyesight. *See* God doing the impossible. Fix your gaze on Him and His unlimited, miracle-working power. Don't question *how* or *when* God will work a miracle on your behalf. Focus your faith until you are fully persuaded—until you are filled with expectation and are praising God for the release of His miracle power *even before* you see a visible manifestation.

It is time for you to break through every hindrance holding you back from walking in the supernatural. You must go beyond your own personal environment. Human reasoning opposes God's purposes and focuses on the impossible. Only when you focus your spiritual eyesight upon the unlimited, mighty God will you begin to live in the realm where nothing is impossible.

I pray for you right now, in the name of Jesus, that the Father will anoint your spiritual eyes so the spiritual cataracts will fall off and you will know what God has planned and purposed for your life. If you have been born again and baptized with the power of the Holy Spirit, you are a supernatural being, filled with the supernatural power of God, created in the image of Christ to do the same mighty works He did. Jesus isn't depending upon your natural abilities, talents, or anything else you possess. He is just looking for those who will act on His promise, *"These signs will follow those who believe..."* (Mark 16:17).

DEVELOPING SUPERNATURAL EYESIGHT

PERSONAL APPLICATION

1. Ask God to give you the ability to see beyond the limitations of the natural into the supernatural realm of the Holy Spirit. Make Paul's prayer in Ephesians 1:17–18 your prayer. Daily ask the Lord to open the eyes of your understanding concerning the circumstances you face. As He begins to open your spiritual eyes to see beyond your situation to His unlimited power, and to see Him working on your behalf, focus your spiritual vision on these things.

2. You may be facing a heavy financial burden; sickness or terminal illness; separation or divorce; or loved ones bound by drugs, alcohol, or other destructive addictions. The moment fear, doubt, worry, or other negative thoughts enter your mind, cast them out and replace them with faith-filled thoughts. Recognize every negative thought of unbelief, fear, or worry as a tool Satan will use to block you from taking hold of your miracle. Cast those thoughts out in Jesus' name and align your thoughts according to the powerful, life-giving force of God's Word and His promises. Begin to speak those promises into your circumstances, and continue to speak them. Fill your mind with thoughts concerning God's awesome might and great love for you.

3. The key to the apostle Paul's supernatural deliverance from prison was that He refused to focus on his circumstances. Knowing God was in control and that

He would deliver him, he praised and worshipped the Lord. In the midst of the circumstances you are currently facing, *begin to praise and worship God,* knowing He will supernaturally intervene and release the miracle you need. Don't wait until you see the manifestation of your miracle. Praise Him, in faith, daily until you see the fulfillment of His promises.

CHAPTER SEVEN

YOUR VITAL LINK TO THE SUPERNATURAL

There is a vital link to the supernatural that will enable you to receive the miracle you need from God. It is a powerful force that God has placed within *all* His sons and daughters and that He wants to release within you. It takes you beyond what your mind can conceive to what He desires to do for you, in you, and through you. It enables you to live in a daily *expectancy* of His miracle provision.

What is this divine link to the supernatural?

It is *hope* that works with faith!

Your level of expectancy must be based on faith and hope that are founded on the only thing in this life that is 100 percent accurate, that never changes, and that has never failed or will fail—the Word of God.

HOPE IS CONFIDENT EXPECTANCY

Biblical hope is different from our everyday use of the word *hope*. Sometimes, we say, "I *hope* this will happen"—meaning we *wish* it would happen, but we really don't expect it to. In contrast, what the Bible means by hope is *"confident expectancy....*Genuine [biblical] hope is not wishful thinking, but a firm assurance about things that are unseen and still in the future."[21]

Biblical hope is therefore not something that depends upon what we perceive with our five natural senses. By its very nature, hope is not based on the way things are today. The Bible says, *"Hope that is* [physically] *seen is no hope at all. Who hopes for what he already has?"* (Romans 8:24 NIV). Instead, it is based on the way things *will* be. Biblical hope has to do with what God has promised in His Word. It works alongside your supernatural eyesight to help you anticipate the fulfillment of His promises and the meeting of your needs.

LIVE IN A DAILY EXPECTANCY OF MIRACLES

Many people consider miracles as the exception, rather than as a normal experience in their lives. But as we have seen, God wants to bring the church into a new spiritual dimension whereby we are looking to Him to perform miracles in our lives on a consistent basis. To do this, we must look to Him daily, *expecting* His miracle provision for all our needs. God doesn't do anything contrary to His nature. When He works miracles in the lives of His children, they are a *natural* flow of His great love for us.

The truth is that a great majority of Christians today are not living on a spiritual level where they are *looking for* a daily manifestation of God's miracle power to flow through their lives. At the first sign of a major sickness, their initial response is to look to the doctors with their medical technologies and abilities instead of looking to God as their ultimate Source of healing. When financial need or crisis comes, their first reaction is to look to the banks and financial institutions instead of looking to God for His supernatural provision. Whenever there is any type of need, the reaction of most Christians is to rely on the natural, instead of believing and expecting God for the supernatural.

God is our Source, and He intends us to look to Him first and foremost in meeting our needs. From cover to cover, the Word of God is filled with promises God has given us that require divine intervention. Why would He have given us so many promises if He did not intend for us to believe and expect Him to work miracles on our behalf?

Are you expecting God to release His supernatural provision into your circumstances?

Earlier, we talked about the fact that there seem to be more miracles taking place overseas than in the United States. The major reason is that their expectancy level is much higher than that of Christians here. In the church in China, Africa, Indonesia, and other parts of the world, there is a dependency on God's miracle provision, and miracles are occurring on a regular basis.

These believers have not been exposed to the humanistic teaching that has influenced the Western church throughout the years. They have not become so self-sufficient that they rely on their natural resources. In many countries, they do not *have* anything else to rely on, and they have learned to trust in

God for His divine intervention in meeting their needs. When the people hear that God wants to perform a miracle of salvation or healing, therefore, they respond in simple, childlike faith, and miracles happen in great numbers on a consistent basis.

The following is an excerpt from a book by Brother Yun, one of the prominent house church leaders in China:

> Many Christians have…asked me why miracles and signs and wonders are so prevalent in China, but not so evident in the West.
>
> In the West you have so much. You have insurance for everything. In a way, you don't need God. When my father was dying of stomach cancer, we sold everything we had to try to cure him. When everything was gone we had no hope but God. We turned to Him in desperation and saw Him mercifully answer our prayers and heal my father. We reasoned that if God could do that then He could do anything, so our faith grew and we've seen many miracles.
>
> In China, the greatest miracles we see are not the healings or other things, but lives transformed by the gospel. We believe we're not called to follow signs and wonders but instead the signs and wonders follow us when the gospel is preached. We don't keep our eyes on the signs and wonders; we keep our eyes on Jesus.
>
> Every house church pastor in China is ready to lay down his life for the gospel. When we live this way, we'll see God do great things by his grace.[22]

YOUR VITAL LINK TO THE SUPERNATURAL

Think about the problems and circumstances you currently face. Are you *expecting* God to release His supernatural provision? Are you eagerly reaching up in childlike hope to God, anticipating that He will give you what you need? Are you living in a daily expectation of miracles? Jesus said, *"If you then, being evil, know how to give good gifts to your children, **how much more** will your Father who is in heaven give good things to those who ask Him!"* (Matthew 7:11, emphasis added).

"How much more"! The Father not only wants us to expect to receive what we need from Him, but He also requires it. *"But without faith it is impossible to please Him, for he who comes to God must believe that He is, and that He is a rewarder of those who diligently seek Him"* (Hebrews 11:6). Our Father is a Rewarder. We must come to Him believing He will do all He has promised.

RAISE YOUR LEVEL OF EXPECTANCY

To walk in the supernatural, therefore, you must *raise* your level of expectancy.

Your level of expectancy is the degree to which you *truly* believe things will happen. There is a natural level of expectancy and a spiritual level of expectancy, and we need to understand the difference. There are people who are considered to be optimistic, who usually have a cheerful outlook on life and expect good things to happen. On the other hand, there are people considered to be pessimistic, who have a tendency to have a sad outlook on life and expect bad things to happen.

In the natural world, a person's expectancy level is based upon their thoughts, emotions, feelings, and what they see

171

and hear. Their sense of expectancy is based upon what they know and anticipate in the natural realm. For example, when harvest time comes, the farmer who has plowed the ground, planted the seed, and properly taken care of the crop expects to reap a good harvest. Yet his level of expectancy depends upon many things. He may expect to reap a small, medium, or large harvest based upon the type of soil, weather, or various other conditions during the year.

> A person's spiritual expectancy level is based upon what he *knows, believes,* and *anticipates* according to God's Word.

In the spiritual realm, a person's expectancy level is not based upon what he thinks, sees, feels, or hears in the natural. It is based upon what he *knows, believes,* and *anticipates* according to God's Word. As we have seen throughout this book, God wants you to break out of the limitations of the natural world. He does not want you to base your level of expectancy on yourself or your ability to think positive. And He does not even want you to base your expectancy of miracles upon your faith alone, but on faith combined with hope.

FAITH IS THE FOUNDATION UPON WHICH HOPE IS BUILT

As you release your faith for the miracle you need, your heart should be filled with hope—an excitement and expectation that you are going to receive it. *"Now faith is the assurance (the confirmation, the title deed) of the things [we] do not see and the conviction of their reality [faith perceiving as real fact what is not revealed to the senses]"* (Hebrews 11:1 AMP). This verse in the King James translation reads, *"Now faith is the substance of things hoped for, the evidence of things not seen"* (Hebrews 11:1). Faith is the *"substance"*—it is not wishful thinking, it is not mere mental belief, but is something substantial that sustains, strengthens, and upholds you.

The Greek word for substance is *hypostasis. Stasis* means "to stand" and *hupo* means "under." The author of the book of Hebrews was saying that faith is the substance, foundation, or ground upon which we build our hope. The apostle Paul wrote,

> *Against all hope, Abraham in hope believed and so became the father of many nations, just as it had been said to him, "So shall your offspring be." Without weakening in his faith, he faced the fact that his body was as good as dead—since he was about a hundred years old—and that Sarah's womb was also dead. Yet he did not waver through unbelief regarding the promise of God, but was strengthened in his faith and gave glory to God, being fully persuaded that God had power to do what he had promised.* (Romans 4:18–21 NIV)

When all hope in the natural was gone, Abraham *"in hope believed."* His faith and hope were released to receive his miracle. In the natural, it was impossible for Abraham to become a father. He was one hundred years old and Sarah was far beyond the age of childbearing. However, against all natural hope and the outward signs and circumstances that regarded it impossible, Abraham, in *hope,* believed.

He did not waver through unbelief regarding God's promise to him. He had a desire stirring within him. He had a living expectation that he would have the son God had told him he would. Through this hope he believed—was *"fully persuaded"*—that God had the power to do what He had promised.

FAITH PERCEIVES THE INVISIBLE, WHILE HOPE REACHES OUT CONFIDENTLY TO RECEIVE

Faith is also evidence. *"Now faith is the substance of things hoped for, the evidence of things not seen"* (Hebrews 11:1 KJV). The word *"evidence"* in the original Greek means "proof; conviction." Faith is proof of the things we desire from God that we do not yet see, and the strong, firm conviction of their reality. *"The proof of things [we] do not see and the conviction of their reality [faith perceiving as real fact what is not revealed to the senses]"* (Hebrews 11:1 AMP).

Faith perceives the things you do not see, that are not revealed to your senses. Hope reaches out with expectation to receive them and counts them as a real fact—a living reality.

Faith envisions the healing you can receive for your body, regardless of what you may be suffering from, such as leukemia, cancer, heart disease, blindness, or deafness. Hope reaches out in earnest expectation to receive and works with your faith to consider that healing to be a reality.

Faith "sees" the financial miracle you can receive. Hope rises up with expectation to meet your faith and considers those finances to be a reality even though you cannot see them and have no idea where they are coming from.

Faith rests upon the fact. Hope expects the fulfillment. It is settled in your mind. There is no doubt, no striving. You rest, knowing it will come to pass.

YOUR VITAL LINK TO THE SUPERNATURAL

BEFORE FAITH IN JESUS CAME

The faith of the Old Testament saints was a simple loyalty to God. It consisted of taking God at His Word and believing His promises. They were so convinced that God could and would fulfill what He had promised that they were filled with hope and acted as if what He had promised had already been accomplished. They had nothing but the promises of God to rest upon, without any visible evidence that those promises would ever be fulfilled, but they regulated the whole course of their lives by those promises.

Yet we have something these faithful saints did not have. The Old Testament prophets believed in God. There were also times when God imparted supernatural faith to them, enabling them to speak a word and cause the Red Sea to part, the sun to stand still, and fire to fall from heaven. God gave

> Hope expects the fulfillment of the spiritual fact that faith perceives as living reality. You rest, knowing that it will come to pass.

them supernatural faith that enabled them to perform mighty miracles and overcome tremendous obstacles. But they did not have the supernatural faith of God *living* in them.

These great miracles were not accomplished through man's own ability to believe, but through a powerful manifestation of the faith *of* God, which came upon men and women who were faithful to Him and believed in Him. God did not depend upon the faith of the great prophets to fulfill His purpose and plan upon the earth. He gave each of them a special manifestation of faith to accomplish what He asked them to do.

Look at Noah's faith:

[Prompted] by faith Noah, being forewarned by God concerning events of which as yet there was no visible sign, took heed and diligently and reverently constructed and prepared an ark for the deliverance of his own family.

(Hebrews 11:7 AMP)

Noah took God at His word. That is what God requires of you today if you are going to take hold of the supernatural. God had forewarned him that He was going to send a great deluge upon the earth—that He was going to cause rain to fall out of the heavens for forty days and forty nights, and that every living thing on the earth would be destroyed.

Noah had a *conviction* of things not seen. Although there had never been a great rain or a flood upon the earth, and there was no visible sign of one, Noah acted in faith upon God's promise and built an ark to preserve himself and his family. His hope was activated, and he expected the floodwaters to come as God had spoken.

Look at Abraham's faith:

[Urged on] by faith Abraham, when he was called, obeyed and went forth to a place which he was destined to receive as an inheritance; and he went, although he did not know or trouble his mind about where he was to go.

(Hebrews 11:8 AMP)

While Abraham was in Mesopotamia, God called him and said, *"Get out of your country and from your relatives, and come to a land that I will show you"* (Acts 7:3). Abraham believed God. His hope or expectation was activated, and he went according to God's word, not knowing where he was going. He responded in implicit faith and obedience to God.

Look at Sarah's faith:

Because of faith also Sarah herself received physical power to conceive a child, even when she was long past the age for it, because she considered [God] Who had given her the promise to be reliable and trustworthy and true to His word. (Hebrews 11:11 AMP)

The *New King James Version* says that Sarah *"judged Him faithful who had promised."* Even though, to the natural mind, it was impossible for Sarah to conceive a child since she was beyond the age of childbearing, through her faith—her unwavering trust and confidence in God's faithfulness to keep His promises—she laid hold of the impossible. Her hope was activated to expect the promised child. As a result, she received strength to conceive.

Look at Joseph's faith:

[Actuated] by faith Joseph, when nearing the end of his life, referred to [the promise of God for] the departure of the Israelites out of Egypt and gave instructions concerning the burial of his own bones. (Hebrews 11:22 AMP)

Joseph had faith in God's promise to bring the Israelites out of Egypt to the Promised Land. He saw it as a real fact. By faith and hope, he took hold of things unseen. Knowing God would fulfill His promise, Joseph gave instructions that his bones should be preserved in Egypt, until the time God delivered them and they would carry his bones with them into Canaan to be buried there.

Look at the faith of the Israelites:

Because of faith the walls of Jericho fell down after they had been encompassed for seven days [by the Israelites].

(Hebrews 11:30 AMP)

God promised the Israelites that the walls of Jericho would *"fall down flat"* (Joshua 6:5) if they would march around the walls once a day for six days, and seven times on the seventh day. The priests were told to carry the ark and blow trumpets made of rams' horns. On the seventh day, in addition to the blowing of the trumpets, all the people were to shout, and when they shouted, the walls of Jericho would fall before them.

Through faith, God's people have subdued kingdoms and obtained promised blessings.

Joshua and the children of Israel believed God would do exactly what He said He would do. To the natural mind, it was an impossibility that the walls of Jericho would fall down due to the Israelites' marching around the walls blowing trumpets and shouting. It was ridiculous. Yet, because of their faith, hope, trust, and reliance upon God's faithfulness to His promises, they obeyed, and the walls fell.

Old Testament prophets and other believers won great victories. They took hold of the miraculous. Hebrews 11:33–34 (AMP, NIV) tells us that they...

- subdued kingdoms.
- obtained promised blessings.
- shut the mouths of lions.
- extinguished the power of raging fire.
- escaped the edge of the sword.
- out of frailty and weakness won strength and became stalwart.
- became powerful in battle.
- routed foreign armies.

Although these Old Testament believers did not receive the fulfillment of the promises of God concerning the Messiah and the kingdom of God (see Hebrews 11:39), they died in faith—a faith that enabled them to see these promises as a reality afar off. Through hope, they expected and were fully persuaded that God would do exactly what He had promised.

> *These people all died controlled and sustained by their faith, but not having received the tangible fulfillment of [God's] promises, only having seen it and greeted it from a great distance by faith.* (Hebrews 11:13 AMP)

The faith of these Old Testament prophets and other believers was powerful, supernatural faith from God that combined with hope so that they lived their lives according to His promises. However, today, we have something even greater than this.

GOD PROVIDED SOMETHING BETTER FOR US

At the conclusion of this great faith chapter of Hebrews 11, we read,

And all of these, though they won divine approval by [means of] their faith, did not receive the fulfillment of what was promised, because God had us in mind and had something better and greater in view for us, so that they [these heroes and heroines of faith] should not come to perfection apart from us.   (Hebrews 11:39–40 AMP)

God has provided something better for us!

The Old Testament saints had faith in God; they believed His promises and trusted in His faithfulness. Through the supernatural faith God imparted to them, they were able to accomplish mighty deeds; they endured torture and affliction and were sustained by their faith and hope. But they did not have the supernatural faith of God that comes through Jesus Christ living in them.

> **We have the supernatural faith of God that comes through Jesus Christ living in us.**

Paul wrote to the Galatians, *"Before faith* [in Jesus Christ] *came, we were kept under guard by the law, kept for the faith which would afterward be revealed"* (Galatians 3:23). True faith had not yet come. The Old Testament prophets and believers had a faith that existed under the law or was supernaturally given by God for a specific purpose. In verse 25, Paul said, *"But after faith has come, we are no longer under a tutor* [the law]."

Faith has come in Christ Jesus! Today we have something better than the Old Testament saints had. We have a supernatural faith *living within us* that is able to make the impossible

possible. Jesus said, *"If you can believe, all things are possible to him who believes"* (Mark 9:23). This supernatural faith enables you to…

- walk by faith, not by sight. (See 2 Corinthians 5:7.)
- quench all the fiery darts of the enemy. (See Ephesians 6:16.)
- overcome the world. (See 1 John 5:4.)

This supernatural faith enables you to live the supernatural life. You may be thinking, *How do I receive this supernatural faith?* or *How can I know that I possess it?*

When you received Jesus, you received His faith. It is in you now, but you must recognize it and learn how to release it in your life.

Many Christians today are still trying to live by their own faith, instead of the supernatural faith of God that is through Jesus. Not knowing how this faith comes, they try to *produce* it. After illustrating the faith of the Old Testament saints, which existed before faith in Christ came, the writer of the book of Hebrews pointed to our source of faith today when he wrote,

> *Therefore we also, since we are surrounded by so great a cloud of witnesses, let us lay aside every weight, and the sin which so easily ensnares us, and let us run with endurance the race that is set before us, looking unto Jesus, the author and finisher of our faith.* (Hebrews 12:1–2)

Jesus is the Source of supernatural faith. He is the Author and Finisher of it.

WALKING IN THE SUPERNATURAL

FOCUS YOUR FAITH AND HOPE

The apostle Paul clearly understood the importance of believers knowing and understanding the "hope" of their calling. He prayed that God would give the Christians in Ephesus a spirit of wisdom and revelation so they would be able to clearly see this hope that was within them. (See Ephesians 1:17–18.) As a child of God, the Father has given you promises that you need to focus your faith and hope upon:

1. The hope of resurrection from the dead. (See, for example, Acts 23:6; 24:15.)
2. The hope of the rapture of the saints. (See 1 Thessalonians 4:16–17.)
3. The hope of the second coming of Christ. (See Titus 2:13.)
4. The hope of the redemption of our bodies. (See, for example, 1 Corinthians 15:51–54.)
5. The hope of reigning with Christ for a thousand years. (See Revelation 20:6.)
6. The hope of eternal life. (See Titus 1:2; 3:7.)

The writer of the book of Hebrews, in commending the Christians for their love and ministry to other believers, urged them to seek the full assurance or fulfillment of their hope: *"And we desire that each one of you show the same diligence to the full assurance of hope until the end"* (Hebrews 6:11). He did not want them to become spiritually lazy when it came to inheriting the promises of God. By maturing in their faith and persevering in their hope, they would be able to *"imitate"* or behave like those who, through *"faith and patience"* (v. 12), were eagerly

182

reaching out in readiness and were receiving the fulfillment of God's promises in their lives.

God wants you to increase and abound in hope: *"Now may the God of hope fill you with all joy and peace in believing, that you may abound in hope by the power of the Holy Spirit"* (Romans 15:13). He wants to release hope within you until it is overflowing in your life. In this verse, we see the key to *how* you will be able to increase your hope and raise your level of expectation. *"By the power of the Holy Spirit"* working in you.

God wants you to *"hold fast"* to your hope.

Accordingly God also, in His desire to show more convincingly and beyond doubt to those who were to inherit the promise the unchangeableness of His purpose and plan, intervened (mediated) with an oath. This was so that, by two unchangeable things [His promise and His oath] in which it is impossible for God ever to prove false or deceive us, we who have fled [to Him] for refuge might have mighty indwelling strength and strong encouragement to grasp and hold fast the hope appointed for us and set before [us].
(Hebrews 6:17–18 AMP)

This hope is a spiritual anchor that will make you immovable! It will enable you to stand firm regardless of the trials and circumstances you face.

[Now] we have this [hope] as a sure and steadfast anchor of the soul [it cannot slip and it cannot break down under whoever steps out upon it—a hope] that reaches farther and enters into [the very certainty of the Presence] within the veil.
(Hebrews 6:19 AMP)

Note that this powerful force of hope brings you into the awesome presence of God and communion with Him!

BASE YOUR HOPE ON THE WRITTEN AND LIVING WORD

Miracles are based upon the *written* and *Living Word* of God—Christ Jesus. In order for you to raise your level of expectation for a miracle, your faith and hope must be firmly rooted and grounded in Christ and the Word of God. You must not look to human beings for a miracle. You must not look to your own level of faith. Your hope and expectation must be centered on Christ and His completed work on the cross.

> **Your need will be met when you release the *faith* and exercise the *hope* God has given you.**

God's Word possesses the power for its own fulfillment. Once you understand that the *same* power that created the heavens and the earth—the sun, the moon, the stars, the flowers, the trees, the animals, and every living thing—is in every promise God has given to you, you will realize that the Word of God is the most powerful force upon the earth today. Its power is not limited by any circumstance you may face. God has spoken a word to meet your situation, and all He requires of you is that you believe what He has spoken will come to pass. You simply need to take the Word that God has spoken and, through the faith of Christ within you, speak forth that Word.

God sent His Living Word into the world for a purpose. *"And the Word became flesh and dwelt among us"* (John 1:14). Jesus came to earth not only to carry your sins and sicknesses on the cross, but also to restore everything that human beings lost as a result of the curse through their disobedience in the garden of Eden. The Living Word came to reinstate humanity to unbroken fellowship and communion with the Father and to set us totally free from all the works of the devil. The Living Word fulfilled His purpose; He defeated Satan once and for all, and then He returned to the Father in heaven. The price has been paid; the work has been done. The Living Word has made it possible for you to have access to all the promises of God contained in His Word.

What does this mean to you as a believer? Whatever circumstance you are facing right now that cannot be met by human means—that requires a supernatural manifestation of God's miracle power—will be met when you release the *faith* and exercise the *hope* God has given you, which are based on the written and Living Word.

Christ has promised that whatever you ask the Father in His name, He will give to you. (See John 15:16.) As you begin to understand that God's Word does not change and that there is absolutely no margin for error, your level of expectancy will be raised. And, as you draw upon the hope God has placed within you, in every circumstance you face, you will *expect* to receive—and through eyes of faith you will see it done!

Hope that works with faith is your link to the supernatural. Take hold of it and begin today to walk in the supernatural, fulfilling all of God's purposes for your life.

PERSONAL APPLICATION

Whatever circumstance you face, are you *expecting* God to release His supernatural provision to meet your need? To raise your level of expectancy, your faith and hope must be firmly rooted and grounded in the living Christ and the Word of God. Determine the promises God has given you in His Word concerning the circumstances you face. Write them down. Focus your faith on these promises. Then, daily expect the fulfillment of them.

Remember that...

FAITH PERCEIVES THE INVISIBLE, WHILE HOPE REACHES OUT CONFIDENTLY TO RECEIVE

Faith perceives the things you do not yet see—healing, financial breakthrough, marriage restoration, deliverance for your rebellious children, salvation of your unsaved loved ones, and so forth.

Hope reaches out with expectation to receive the miracle and considers it a real fact, although you do not see it in the natural.

Once you have released your faith, and hope has risen up to meet it, rest in the fact, knowing that what you are believing and expecting will come to pass.

CHAPTER EIGHT

POSSESSING GOD'S DNA

As a child of God, you possess His DNA.

What is God's DNA? How will it enable you to walk in the supernatural? The answers to these questions will help you take another step forward in learning how to live a life where God's miracle power is flowing through you on a consistent basis.

Human DNA is referred to as the molecule of heredity. It is responsible for the genetic propagation of most inherited traits. During reproduction, DNA is replicated and transmitted to the offspring. It is possible to determine the father of a child by comparing their DNA. The DNA clearly identifies the child as being the father's offspring.

Similarly, God's children possess His DNA—His "seed"—which identifies them as belonging to Him. That seed is incorruptible. We are *"born again, not of corruptible seed but incorruptible, **through the word of God** which lives and abides forever"* (1 Peter 1:23, emphasis added). Jesus is the Living Word who comes to live within us when we are born again. The Greek word used for *"incorruptible"* in this verse is *apathartos,* meaning "not liable to corruption or decay." *Merriam-Webster's 11th Collegiate Dictionary* defines *incorruptible* as "not subject to decay or dissolution," and "incapable of being bribed or morally corrupted."

God's seed is incorruptible—it is absolutely holy, pure, and incapable of moral decay. His DNA in His true sons and daughters is immortal and imperishable; it cannot be destroyed. It is this holy seed that has the power to transform and conform you into the image of Christ.

> **The single characteristic that will clearly identify the true end-time church is that it will be holy.**

God's DNA—His very life—is within you so that Christ's perfect, sinless life will be reproduced in you. *"For whom He foreknew, He also predestined to be conformed to the image of His Son, that He might be the firstborn among many brethren"* (Romans 8:29).

When we possess God's DNA, therefore, we no longer habitually practice sin.

> *No one born (begotten) of God [deliberately, knowingly, and habitually] practices sin, for God's nature ["seed" NKJV] abides in him [His principle of life, the divine sperm, remains permanently within him]; and he cannot practice sinning because he is born (begotten) of God. By this it is made clear who take their nature from God and are His children and who take their nature from the devil and are his children: no one who does not practice righteousness [who does not conform to God's will in purpose, thought,*

and action] is of God; neither is anyone who does not love
his brother (his fellow believer in Christ).

(1 John 3:9–10 AMP)

John said that no one who is truly born of God, having His DNA, will make a habit of sinning. This doesn't mean it is impossible for a Christian to commit sin. John earlier wrote, *"I write this to you so that you will not sin. But if anybody does sin, we have one who speaks to the Father in our defense—Jesus Christ, the Righteous One"* (1 John 2:1 NIV). If we do sin, we are to immediately repent, ask God's forgiveness through Christ, and move forward. Yet those who are living and abiding in Christ, with His Word living in them, will no longer *regularly* practice sinning. Notice carefully the reason why: *"for God's nature abides in him [His principle of life, the divine sperm, remains permanently within him]; and he cannot practice sinning because he is born (begotten) of God"* (1 John 3:9 AMP).

The coming, awesome release of God's miracle power through the church will be the result of the dedication and consecration of righteous, sold-out believers who reflect His nature. The one outstanding characteristic that will clearly identify the true end-time church is that it will be holy.

When Christ laid down His life for the church, His ultimate purpose was that, at the end of the age, He would present the church to Himself, pure and blameless, as a bride adorned for her husband in all her splendor.

Christ also loved the church and gave Himself for her, that
He might sanctify and cleanse her with the washing of water
by the word, that He might present her to Himself a glorious

church, not having spot or wrinkle or any such thing, but that she should be holy and without blemish.

(Ephesians 5:25–27)

As a child of God who possesses God's DNA, you are called to be holy. *"But just as he who called you is holy, so be holy in all you do; for it is written: 'Be holy, because I am holy'"* (1 Peter 1:15–16 NIV).

A CALL FOR TRUE HOLINESS

One of the reasons why we do not see more of God's power manifested in the church today is that there is a lack of true holiness. There are many good works being done in the name of Jesus. Many believers are working diligently in ministry outreaches, and outwardly they are successful. However, the real, lasting fruit that results from a life of true holiness is often missing.

We are living in a day when sin, lust, immorality, violence, perversion, hate, and greed have multiplied to such a great extent that our cities have become modern-day Sodoms and Gomorrahs. People are not only fulfilling the desires of their evil imaginations, but they are also flaunting them and seeking to establish their ungodly practices as accepted, normal ways of living. Tragically, many Christians are being drawn into the thinking and behavior of the world.

In this coming move of God within the church, there will be a cleansing and call for true holiness among His people *before* the release of His supernatural power. We must prepare to walk through a season of fire—of spiritual refining, purifying, cleansing.

The Scripture says, *"Our God is a consuming fire"* (Hebrews 12:29). A fire is going to burn. It will intensify and burn throughout the church until everything that is not of God is consumed. As Head of His church, Christ is coming to restore divine order and divine authority.

I believe therefore that a revival of repentance and restoration is coming to the church. Two streams of the Spirit will come together—the stream of the fire of Christ purging His church, and the stream of the supernatural power of God.

As we face the final countdown before Christ's return and begin to experience the refining fire of Christ in our lives, we must have a new, fresh revelation of Christ, so we may see Him as He is. When Christ returns to this earth, He is not coming as the meek, mild Savior but as a warrior in flaming fires of judgment upon the wicked. Paul wrote to the believers in Thessalonica, *"...when the Lord Jesus is revealed from heaven with His mighty angels, in flaming fire taking vengeance on those who do not know God, and on those who do not obey the gospel of our Lord Jesus Christ"* (2 Thessalonians 1:7–8).

> **Don't run away from the fire—run *to* it! There is intimacy and there is power in the fire.**

Christ will cleanse and prepare the church so that we will not be consumed by the fires of judgment. Do not be deceived. Christ is coming in power and great glory to claim a bride who is holy. We do not have time to play church. Religious systems are coming under this fire. The book of Acts, beginning with the second chapter, is a record of how the Holy Spirit and the fire of God swept through the religious establishment of Judaism in the first century and brought about a spiritual revolution. The fire of God purified the early church with the judgment that came upon Ananias and Sapphira for lying to God. Following this, great signs and wonders and healings were manifested through the apostles. (See Acts 5:1–16.) This same fire is coming to burn through the religious systems and hypocrisy of our day. The purpose of this fire is to…

- purify and cleanse.
- reveal sin and burn it out.
- separate the "chaff" from the "wheat" [false believers from true believers].
- bring judgment upon those who refuse to repent.

The fire that is coming to the church will burn through the exterior of our lives to expose and reveal the deepest attitudes that lie inside the innermost recesses of our beings. Nothing will be hidden from God.

In the midst of this wicked generation, God has set you apart to be holy to Him. In your quest to walk in the supernatural, you must be willing to submit yourself to the purifying fire of the Holy Spirit and cry out for God to purge everything in your life that is displeasing to Him.

Don't run away from the fire—run *to* it!

There is intimacy in the fire. And there is power in the fire.

GOD'S HOLY SEED IS PRODUCING HIS LIFE IN YOU

To live, walk, and operate in the supernatural power of almighty God, you must live a life separated from sin and set apart for God. This involves every aspect of your life, including your thoughts, actions, conversations, and relationships. God's holy seed—His spiritual DNA—is reproducing in you...

- His love.
- His joy.
- His peace.
- His mercy.
- His faith.
- His power.
- His glory.
- His holiness.
- His image.
- His life!

Think about what this means to you. Through Christ, the holy seed of God has been placed within you to produce a new life—a new nature that is *"created in God's image, [Godlike] in true righteousness and holiness"* (Ephesians 4:24 AMP).

To walk in the supernatural, with His power and glory manifested in your life, you must therefore walk in true holiness. Notice I qualified my statement by using the words *"true holiness."* I am not referring to a legalistic, outward observance based upon man-made doctrines. True holiness originates from God and is the result of Christ's life being manifested in our lives so that we are walking in His righteousness. The apostle John made this point crystal clear when he said, *"Little children, let no one deceive you. He who practices righteousness is righteous, just as* [Jesus] *is righteous"* (1 John 3:7).

WALKING IN THE SUPERNATURAL

The Scriptures admonish us to *"pursue...holiness, without which no one will see the Lord"* (Hebrews 12:14). Earlier, I referenced 1 Peter 1:15–16, in which Peter quoted this divine command from our heavenly Father: *"Be holy, for I am the Lord your God"* (Leviticus 20:7). God will not release His power and glory through unclean vessels. That is why it is so important that we have a fresh revelation of this great truth: the holy seed of almighty God is in all His true sons and daughters, making it possible for them to live a holy life and to walk in the supernatural. John taught,

> *You know that He [Jesus] appeared in visible form and became Man to take away [upon Himself] sins, and in Him there is no sin [essentially and forever]. No one who abides in Him [who lives and remains in communion with and in obedience to Him—deliberately, knowingly, and habitually] commits (practices) sin. No one who [habitually] sins has either seen or known Him [recognized, perceived, or understood Him, or has had an experiential acquaintance with Him].* (1 John 3:5–6 AMP)

You have been born of God, and His holy seed is in you. From the beginning, God the Father planned to have sons and daughters, created in His own image and likeness,

- who are loving as He is loving.
- who are merciful as He is merciful.
- who are forgiving as He is forgiving.
- who are holy even as He is holy.
- who walk in the same power and authority that Jesus did.

POSSESSING GOD'S DNA

Even before the foundation of the world, God purposed to have a *holy* people—unlike those with the mind-set and motivations of the world—who would be consecrated to Him. He planned to live within His holy people and accomplish His purposes on earth through them. The apostle Paul, writing to the believers in Ephesus, said,

> *[In His love] He chose us [actually picked us out for Himself as His own] in Christ before the foundation of the world, that we should be holy (consecrated and set apart for Him) and blameless in His sight, even above reproach, before Him in love.* (Ephesians 1:4 AMP)

The Greek word for *"holy"* in this verse is *hagios*, which means "to be separated from sin and consecrated or set apart for God." The word *"blameless"* is translated from the Greek word *anomos*, meaning "free from blemish."

Similarly, in writing to the Thessalonians, Paul said, *"For God did not call us to uncleanness, but in holiness"* (1 Thessalonians 4:7). He also told Timothy, *"[God] has saved us and called us with a holy calling"* (2 Timothy 1:9).

The apostle Peter expressed the same concept. God has called us out and set us apart as *"a holy priesthood, to offer up spiritual sacrifices acceptable to God through Jesus Christ"* (1 Peter 2:5). He has made us *"a royal priesthood, a holy nation"* (v. 9).

FIX YOUR GAZE ON GOD, WHO ALONE IS HOLY

To fully understand what holiness is, and what it means to be holy as God is holy, we must fix our gaze upon our heavenly Father. Holiness is the divine essence of God in His infinite perfection. The Scriptures tell us that, night and day, the four heavenly creatures around the throne of God cry out, *"Holy, holy, holy, Lord God Almighty, who was and is and is to come!"* (Revelation 4:8). His entire nature is holy. *"The LORD is righteous in all his ways, and holy in all his works"* (Psalm 145:17 KJV). God's love is holy; His justice and judgments are holy; His grace is holy; His mercy, patience, and lovingkindness are holy.

Sinful flesh cannot stand in God's holy presence. *"[God] only hath immortality, dwelling in the light which no man can approach unto; whom no man hath seen, nor can see: to whom be honour and power everlasting"* (1 Timothy 6:16 KJV). No one can see God face-to-face and live. (See Exodus 33:20.) Man's sinful flesh would be consumed by His glorious holiness.

> From the beginning, the Father planned to have sons and daughters, created in His own image and likeness.

In His first commands to the Israelites, God revealed His holy nature. He taught that everything around Him and all who would come near Him must be holy. He made it clear that He would dwell only in the midst of holiness. Consequently, the Old Testament tabernacle and everything in it, such as the priests, the altar, the sacrifices, the oil, and the bread, had to be holy. It was in the Holy of Holies that God especially revealed Himself as the Holy One. The veil before the Holy of Holies separated Him from human beings in their sinful state.

The judgments of God recorded in His Word give us a glimpse of His holiness and hatred of sin. When Aaron's sons, Nadab and Abihu, offered unauthorized fire upon the altar, contrary to God's command, fire came out from the presence of the Lord and consumed them. (See Leviticus 10:1–2; Exodus 30:9–10.) There were specific instructions concerning what was to be offered on the altar and how. Nadab and Abihu's action was a blatant rebellion against God and a profaning of the Holy Place. When Aaron approached Moses concerning God's judgment upon his sons, Moses said, *"This is what the LORD spoke, saying: 'By those who come near Me I must be regarded as holy; and before all the people I must be glorified'"* (Leviticus 10:3).

GOD'S PRESENCE MAKES HOLY

Moses first saw the Lord, the Holy One, in a fiery bush that was not consumed.

> *And the Angel of the LORD appeared to him in a flame of fire from the midst of a bush. So he looked, and behold, the bush was burning with fire, but the bush was not consumed. Then Moses said, "I will now turn aside and see this great sight, why the bush does not burn." So when the LORD saw that he turned aside to look, God called to him from the midst of the bush and said, "Moses, Moses!" And he said, "Here I am." Then He said, "Do not draw near this place. Take your sandals off your feet, for the place where you stand is holy ground."* (Exodus 3:2–5)

At that moment, Moses sensed the awesome holiness of almighty God and hid his face in fear. *"And Moses hid his face, for he was afraid to look upon God"* (v. 6).

Why was the ground where Moses stood holy ground? Because where God is, there is holiness. The very place where Moses stood was made holy by His presence.

Notice that the first impression God's holiness produced in Moses was that of fear and awe. This sense of sin and unfitness to stand in God's presence is the foundation of true knowledge and worship of Him.

Have you ever wondered why God told Moses to take off his sandals? I believe the sandals represent an attachment and love for the world. When we stand in His holy presence, all that must be put off. We must come before God stripped of every covering of the flesh and bow before Him in His holy presence.

> **None of the works we do makes us righteous or holy. Our holiness is in Christ *by faith.***

The presence of God in the midst of His people today causes us to walk on "holy ground." To an even greater degree, His presence makes holy the place where He lives and takes up His permanent habitation—us!

Isaiah saw a vision of the Lord seated on a throne, high and exalted, in all His glorious splendor. Above His throne were seraphim, each having six wings. One of the seraphim cried out in a loud voice, *"Holy, holy, holy is the LORD of hosts"* (Isaiah 6:3). Isaiah saw the temple filled with smoke, and he cried out, *"Woe is me, for I am undone! Because I am a man of unclean lips, and I dwell in the midst of a people of unclean lips; for my eyes have seen the King, the LORD of hosts"* (v. 5).

When God called Isaiah as a prophet to the nation of Israel, he was of the nobility and a recognized statesman. He was a man of great integrity and was considered the most righteous man in the nation. Yet, when he saw the absolute holiness of God, he saw himself as he really was—corrupt and undone. As

Paul wrote, *"There is none righteous, no, not one"* (Romans 3:10). Isaiah gazed upon the holiness of God, and his spirit was exposed and laid bare before Him. He realized the depth of his own sinful nature and was overwhelmed by what he saw. He saw the awfulness of his sin and the sins of the people.

With great fear and trembling, Isaiah said, *"Woe is me, for I am undone!"* (Isaiah 6:5). He did not make excuses. He did not try to justify himself or establish his own righteousness. But God sent one of the seraphim with a live burning coal from His holy altar; the seraph touched it to Isaiah's lips, cleansing him from his sins. (See verses 6–7.)

This is the type of revelation we must have today. Like Isaiah, we need to see God in His holiness. We need to see His purity and His hatred for sin. Then, as we get a glimpse of His great holiness, we will be stripped bare of our own self-righteousness. We will be humbled in His mighty presence, and we will recognize the sin and unrighteousness in our lives and our great need of cleansing.

GOD WILL MANIFEST HIS POWER THROUGH A HOLY PEOPLE

Only as we look into God's *absolute holiness* will we begin to weep, mourn, and repent for the sin that has entered the church. Only then will we be able to cry out for Him to take live coals from His holy altar, touch our lips, and burn out all the sin and impurities in our lives, until we are able to stand in His presence thoroughly cleansed and made whole. Only then will we begin to cry out to Him for mercy concerning the gross immorality and sin that surrounds us in our communities and cities.

It was not until *after* his revelation of the holiness of God, and a time of cleansing and consecration, that God commissioned Isaiah and sent him as a prophet with a message to the people. (See Isaiah 6:9.) God alone is holy, and only His indwelling presence in our lives makes us holy. Andrew Murray summed up true holiness in this way: "Not what I am or do or give is holiness, but what God is and gives and does to me. It is God's taking possession of me that makes me holy." [23]

Again, none of the works we do makes us righteous or holy. Our holiness is in Christ *by faith*. The apostle Paul's deepest desire was, *"That I may gain Christ and be found in Him, not having my own righteousness, which is from the law, but that which is through - faith in Christ, the righteousness which is from God by faith"* (Philippians 3:8–9). God's call to the church today is, *"Be holy, for I am holy"* (1 Peter 1:16). As we respond by surrendering all that we are to Him, He will take full possession of us by His Spirit.

To be holy and walk in the supernatural, you cannot allow unconfessed sin to remain in your life. It is up to you. You cannot compromise with the world's standards or live your life to satisfy the carnal, sinful desires of your flesh. God has made you His holy habitation. Once more, Paul said,

For the temple of God is holy, which temple you are.

(1 Corinthians 3:17)

Do you not know that your body is the temple of the Holy Spirit who is in you, whom you have from God, and you are not your own? For you were bought at a price; therefore glorify God in your body and in your spirit, which are God's.

(1 Corinthians 6:19–20)

POSSESSING GOD'S DNA

You are no longer your own. You belong to God.

You have been bought with a great price.

You possess God's DNA.

Knowing these things, you must no longer live your life simply to please yourself, or live according to your own will. You must pursue holiness (see Hebrews 12:14), and perfect your holiness. (See 2 Corinthians 7:11.) How? By dedicating your whole being—spirit, soul, and body—to God. Through the blood of Jesus, you have been made holy and blameless—separated from sin and consecrated to God. Through Him, you have the ability to live a righteous, holy life. However, you must exercise your will to obey God and crucify the lusts of your flesh. Where once you exercised your will to sin, you are now able, through the

> **Many Christians have substituted familiarity with God for intimacy with Him.**

power of the Holy Spirit, to exercise your will to say no to sin and walk in obedience to Christ.

This means you don't have to yield to the temptations of the flesh. You don't have to be ruled by worldly habits and desires. You don't have to yield to impure thoughts, an unruly temper, or an uncontrolled tongue. Paul said, *"But now that you have been set free from sin and have become slaves to God, the benefit you reap leads to holiness, and the result is eternal life"* (Romans 6:22 NIV).

In this coming great move of the Spirit, God will raise up men and women all over the world, and in every sphere of activity, who will manifest His holiness. As they dedicate and consecrate themselves, and walk in holiness before Him, He will use them to manifest His power and glory to the world through great signs and wonders. Holy men and women will speak forth the message God has placed within their hearts.

SIX KEYS TO WALKING IN HOLINESS

Based on what we have just learned, here are six keys to walking in the holiness God has made possible by His Spirit living and working in you.

1. RECEIVE A FRESH REVELATION OF GOD'S HOLINESS

To walk in the supernatural power of God, you must personally have a fresh revelation of Him in His holiness. In our limited human understanding, it is impossible to fully comprehend the depth and greatness of His holiness. But we must have a spiritual breakthrough by which God reveals His holiness to us by His Spirit.

A great majority of Christians today have lost sight of God's holiness, purity, and righteousness. *They have substituted familiarity with God for intimacy with Him.* They see God as a "Daddy" who will turn His head when they sin. They think they will not be punished, but that they can continue sinning and He will pat them on their heads and send them on their way.

They are missing an awesome, reverential fear of God.

Instead of hating sin as God hates sin, the church has become comfortable with it. Rather than taking a firm stand and boldly speaking out against sin, without a fear of man, we gloss over it. We cover it up. We ignore it. Our pulpits are filled with ministers who are continually preaching grace, love, and mercy but are neglecting to tell people that God is also a *holy* God who hates sin and will not allow their sins to go unpunished, if they do not repent and turn away from them.

If ever we needed to have a fresh revelation of the holiness of God, it is today. We must have this revelation until we are willing to rid ourselves of all self-righteousness and hypocrisy and allow God to reveal to us the sin in our lives. If we are to walk in His holiness, manifesting His supernatural miracle power, we must have a holy fear that trembles at the very thought of grieving the Father by our sins, and a deep longing to dwell in His holy presence.

2. PURSUE HOLINESS

"Pursue peace with all people, and holiness, without which no one will see the Lord" (Hebrews 12:14). Knowing that God requires holiness and has said that without holiness no one will see Him, you must make holiness a priority in your life.

Living a holy life is not something that will automatically happen as a result of accepting Christ and being born again. Although you possess God's DNA, you must understand His provision for you to walk in holiness before Him, and earnestly *pursue* holiness.

Whenever an athlete sets his goal on obtaining an Olympic gold medal, he doesn't just sit around waiting until the day he competes, expecting the prize to suddenly fall into his lap. He pursues his goal, exerting every possible effort, making whatever sacrifices of time and energy are necessary until the day his goal becomes a reality and he takes hold of that gold medal.

Well-known champion cyclist Lance Armstrong was the first man to win a seventh consecutive victory in the Tour de France, a feat unequalled in the race's over one-hundred-year history.

When he was just twenty-five, Lance was diagnosed with advanced testicular cancer that had spread to his lungs and brain. He underwent several operations and four cycles of chemotherapy and fought back—not just to recovery, but also to his first Tour de France win in 1999.

> **If ever we needed to have a fresh revelation of the holiness of God, it is today.**

Armstrong attributes his success to a brutally punishing training regime, absolute fitness, dedication, and the mental will to win that came from his battle against cancer. He pursued the prize by exerting every possible effort to obtain it. The apostle Paul wrote, *"I **press** toward the goal for the prize of the upward call of God in Christ Jesus"* (Philippians 3:14, emphasis added). In other words, like Lance Armstrong or any other athlete running a race to win, Paul was *spiritually striving,* focusing his eyes on the goal and exerting the greatest possible effort to win the race and obtain the prize.

Spiritual striving. This is the type of energy that you must put forth, through the power of the Holy Spirit within you, to pursue holiness.

3. PUT OFF THE OLD MAN AND PUT ON THE NEW

To be holy and walk in the supernatural, you must continually *"put off"* or rid yourself of your *"old man"* (Ephesians

4:22)—your old habits, carnal thoughts, fleshly desires, old ways of living. Then you must *"put on the new man"*—with its holy desires, thoughts, attitudes, manner of speech, and actions—*"which was created according to God, in true righteousness and holiness"* (v. 24).

We have been made holy through Christ's precious blood. His work is finished. No further sacrifice is necessary. Nothing had been left undone. It is by faith in His finished work that we are made righteous and are able to walk in holiness before Him.

> *And in accordance with this will [of God] we have been made holy (consecrated and sanctified) through the offering made once for all of the body of Jesus Christ (the Anointed One).…For by a single offering He has forever completely cleansed and perfected those who are consecrated and made holy.* (Hebrews 10:10, 14 AMP)

Although we have already been made holy, it is very clear that the Father expects His true sons and daughters to *live* in that holiness by crucifying the works of the flesh and putting on the new man.

Put off the old and put on the new. *"Be* [constantly] *renewed in the spirit of your mind"* (Ephesians 4:23). Paul emphasized this process when writing to the church in Colossae:

> *Put to death, therefore, whatever belongs to your earthly nature: sexual immorality, impurity, lust, evil desires and greed, which is idolatry. Because of these, the wrath of God is coming. You used to walk in these ways, in the life you once lived. But now you must rid yourselves of all such things*

as these: anger, rage, malice, slander, and filthy language from your lips. Do not lie to each other, since you have taken off your old self with its practices and have put on the new self, which is being renewed in knowledge in the image of its Creator. (Colossians 3:5–10 NIV)

He also wrote to the Ephesian church, *"Get rid of all bitterness, rage and anger, brawling and slander, along with every form of malice"* (Ephesians 4:31 NIV). He revealed that it is up to you, through the power of the Holy Spirit,

- *to strip yourself* of your old, unregenerate nature.
- *to crucify—put to death*—the carnal desires of your flesh.
- *to be constantly renewed* in the spirit of your mind.
- *to put on the new nature*, which is being renewed in knowledge in the image of its Creator.

All these are your responsibility; God expects you to do them by the power of His Spirit living in you.

Are you willing to pay the price to walk in holiness and God's supernatural power? There are Christians who cannot control their bad tempers, who have jealousy, unforgiveness, hatred, and bitterness in their hearts. There are Christians who struggle with ungodly desires. Instead of acting in faith on the Word, they are waiting for God to do all the work—to take away every evil habit and desire of their flesh.

Through Christ, you are set free from Satan's grip and the power of sin. The holy seed is working in you to produce the life of God, *"created in God's image, [Godlike] in true righteousness and holiness"* (Ephesians 4:24 AMP). Through the power of the Holy Spirit, you must put to death carnal desires and the works of your flesh, and put on the new man.

4. DEDICATE AND CONSECRATE YOURSELF AS A HOLY SACRIFICE TO GOD

As a redeemed child of God, you owe a debt to dedicate and consecrate your entire being as a holy sacrifice to Him. Paul wrote,

> *I appeal to you therefore, brethren, and beg of you in view of [all] the mercies of God, to make a decisive dedication of your bodies [presenting all your members and faculties] as a living sacrifice, holy (devoted, consecrated) and well pleasing to God, which is your reasonable (rational, intelligent) service and spiritual worship. Do not be conformed to this world (this age), [fashioned after and adapted to its external, superficial customs], but be transformed (changed) by the [entire] renewal of your mind [by its new ideals and its new attitude], so that you may prove [for yourselves] what is the good and acceptable and perfect will of God, even the thing which is good and acceptable and perfect [in His sight for you].* (Romans 12:1–2 AMP)

To walk in holiness, you must make a decision that you will daily surrender yourself to God and let the Holy Spirit work in you, putting to death the works of the flesh. Again, it is impossible to live a holy life in your own strength. You must depend upon the Holy Spirit and yield yourself fully, allowing Him to convict you of sin and all unrighteousness.

God has sent the fire of His Spirit into our spirits. As a consuming fire, it is to continually burn within us, purging and cleansing away the sin and making us living sacrifices that are holy and acceptable to God.

As I said earlier, Jesus is going to visit His church, and the self-serving attitudes and self-centeredness will be exposed and burnt out. The true motivations of men's hearts will be revealed, and man-made kingdoms will be torn down. Preachers' egos will be torn down. The fire will reveal everything in the lives of God's true sons and daughters that has not yet been crucified.

> As the fire of God burns within us, we will walk in His righteousness and power.

When this fire comes to you, there will not be a motive, an attitude, or an action that will be hidden. Everything that should have been crucified with Jesus—that has not died, that you are still holding on to—will be revealed.

Are you ready for Him to come to you? Are you willing to submit yourself to Christ's refining fire? To prepare to walk in this season of fire, you must…

- Recognize the lateness of the hour and hear what the Spirit of God is saying to His church.
- Humble yourself and be willing to stand before God spiritually naked—stripped of your spiritual pride.
- Be willing to yield to His Spirit, repent, and allow Christ to burn everything out of your life that is displeasing to Him.

Our lives are to be set on fire by the Holy Spirit, where His presence within us is a *consuming fire!* When we yield to Him, this holy fire will burn away self and give us a holy, burning passion for the lost. As this fire burns within us, we will walk in righteousness before God, and His power will be released in us as it was through the believers in the early church. The Spirit within us will be like a fire that cannot be contained or extinguished. Wherever we go, His power and glory will be manifested through us. The cry of our hearts in the days to come must be, "O God, consume us with Your fire. Set us on fire with Your Spirit!"

5. SEE SIN AS GOD SEES IT AND KEEP YOURSELF UNDEFILED

When you truly get a glimpse of the Father and His absolute holiness, and understand that He has placed His holy seed within you—making it possible for you to be holy even as He is holy—you begin to see sin as He does, and to hate it as He does.

There are ministers in our pulpits who have left their wives for other women and think nothing of it. There are others who are secretly addicted to pornography and other lusts of the flesh. Our churches are filled with Christians who are living double lives. On the outside, they look holy. They attend church regularly, pray, and seem to observe the rules of conduct established by their churches or denominations. But they allow their minds to be filled with unholy thoughts and attitudes, such as…

- lust;
- jealousy;
- fear, doubt, and unbelief;
- anger, hatred, unforgiveness, and bitterness;

- covetousness and greed;
- pride and selfishness.

Not only must we hate the sin—such as violence, greed, homosexuality, abortion, murder, and child abuse—that surrounds us in the world, but we must also hate with an intense hatred any sin that would defile or contaminate us. We are to *"abhor what is evil. Cling to what is good"* (Romans 12:9). We are to shudder at sin and turn away from it in disgust, *"hating even the garment defiled by the flesh"* (Jude 23). To walk in the holy presence of God, we are to *"abstain from all appearance of evil"* (1 Thessalonians 5:22 KJV). We are to keep ourselves away from anything that looks like sin, leads to sin, is questionable, or borders on sin.

> *"You are the temple of the living God."*
> —2 Corinthians 6:16

Those who continue to habitually sin against God will not enter into heaven and live in His presence, but will one day be judged and *"will be cast out into outer darkness. There will be weeping and gnashing of teeth"* (Matthew 8:12). Uncleanness is one of the works of the flesh, and Paul warned the Galatians, *"Those who practice such things will not inherit the kingdom of God"* (Galatians 5:21). He also told the Ephesians, *"For this you know, that no fornicator, unclean person, nor covetous man, who is an idolater, has any inheritance in the kingdom of Christ and God"* (Ephesians 5:5).

Christians who think they are hiding their sins from God or that their sins will go unpunished (unless they repent of them) are deceived.

POSSESSING GOD'S DNA

Do not be deceived, God is not mocked; for whatever a man sows, that he will also reap. For he who sows to his flesh will of the flesh reap corruption, but he who sows to the Spirit will of the Spirit reap everlasting life. (Galatians 6:7–8)

Knowing that Jesus died to cleanse you from all sin and that He is coming for a church that is without spot or blemish, you must hate every sin that would keep you from walking pure and holy before Him. You must keep yourself unspotted from worldly attitudes and actions.

Pure and undefiled religion before God and the Father is this: to visit orphans and widows in their trouble, and to keep oneself unspotted from the world. (James 1:27)

The call of the Spirit to those who are hungry to walk in the supernatural power of God is, *"Be separate....Do not touch what is unclean"*:

And what agreement has the temple of God with idols? For you are the temple of the living God. As God has said: "I will dwell in them and walk among them. I will be their God, and they shall be My people." Therefore "Come out from among them and be separate, says the Lord. Do not touch what is unclean, and I will receive you. I will be a Father to you, and you shall be My sons and daughters, says the Lord Almighty." (2 Corinthians 6:16–18)

"Unclean" in this verse is translated from the Greek word *akathartos*, which refers to that which is impure, morally unclean, defiled, and filthy. This doesn't mean you are to separate yourself from unbelievers and the sin that is in the world by going somewhere out into the desert or into the mountains to live in

seclusion. Yet, in the midst of this sin-infested world, God is calling you to separate yourself from everything that would defile and contaminate you and to set yourself apart in consecration to Him. As a people whom God has called to be holy and blameless, we are not to become involved with any of those things in our world today that are unclean, impure, immoral, and unholy.

The apostle John said, *"All unrighteousness is sin"* (1 John 5:17). Sin is lawlessness, a rejection of the will of God and a substitution of the will of self. It is every act of disobedience to God's Word. To walk in holiness, you must continually submit yourself to the Holy Spirit and allow Him to convict you of any and all sin in your life. You must be quick both to recognize any sin and repent of it.

As the church returns to holiness, God will cleanse, heal, and restore His people.

The penetrating, piercing gaze of Christ's eyes is upon the church, and He sees the seducing spirits that have infiltrated it. There is a spirit of adultery, a spirit of fornication, a spirit of uncleanliness and ungodliness among His people today. If we were truly walking in the fear of God, there would be no compromising Christians seeking worldly pleasures and fulfilling the lusts of their flesh. Christians wouldn't be living to please self instead of seeking God and following Him in obedience. If we had a hatred for sin, there would be no hypocrisy, greed, or covetousness among those claiming to be born-again Christians. If we had a hatred for sin, instead of "sweeping sin under the carpet," as the church has been doing, we would be exposing it and calling for true repentance.

The time has come for the church to speak out against the sins that have entered it. Pastors, I urge you to take a strong stand against sin and call people to repentance. Call them to come before God and pray through until they are cleansed and have the power, through the Holy Spirit, to crucify their evil desires and to live a holy, victorious life.

We cannot afford to halfheartedly prepare ourselves for Christ's coming or take lightly what the Father has revealed to us in His Word—that we must be holy as He is holy and *"pursue...holiness, without which no one will see the Lord"* (Hebrews 12:14). God has not changed His mind about sin. His Word hasn't changed. The wages of sin is still death. (See Romans 6:23.) We must not waste any time but do everything within our power to separate ourselves from all that is unrighteous. The apostle Peter said,

> *But the day of the Lord will come as a thief in the night, in which the heavens will pass away with a great noise, and the elements will melt with fervent heat; both the earth and the works that are in it will be burned up. Therefore, since all these things will be dissolved, what manner of persons ought you to be in holy conduct and godliness?...We, according to His promise, look for new heavens and a new earth in which righteousness dwells. Therefore, beloved, looking forward to these things, be diligent to be found by Him in peace, without spot and blameless.*
>
> (2 Peter 3:10–11, 13–14)

Peter said to *"be diligent"*—to make every effort—*"to be found...without spot and blameless"* at Christ's coming. *Merriam-Webster's 11th Collegiate Dictionary* defines *diligent* as "characterized by steady, earnest, and energetic effort: painstaking."

WALKING IN THE SUPERNATURAL

To walk in the supernatural, you must live your life in the holy fear of the Lord and not be lax in your dedication and commitment to walk in holiness. You must not become so caught up with the cares of this world that you fail to prepare yourself for that awesome day when you will stand before Him. Instead, you must be diligent through painstaking, steady, earnest, and energetic effort. You must spiritually strive to pursue holiness. Jesus said, *"Strive to enter through the narrow gate"* (Luke 13:24). Again, you can do this by continually humbling yourself before the Lord and allowing Him to reveal the sin and impurities in your life and everything that is displeasing to Him. You can draw upon the power of the Holy Spirit to bring your entire being into submission to God and His Word.

HE WHO BEGAN THE WORK IN YOU WILL BRING IT TO COMPLETION

As you pursue holiness, remember that the Father has placed His DNA within you and will cause His seed to reproduce His life in you. Paul wrote,

> *I am convinced and sure of this very thing, that He Who began a good work in you will continue until the day of Jesus Christ [right up to the time of His return] developing [that good work] and perfecting and bringing it to full completion in you.* (Philippians 1:6 AMP)

During the coming great move of God, as the church returns to holiness, God will cleanse, heal, and restore His people to a position of power. When you begin to dedicate yourself to holiness, where you are practicing holiness in every area of your life, God will revive your spirit and manifest His

214

power and glory in a greater measure than you have ever experienced.

Receive this promise deep into your spirit:

For thus says the High and Lofty One who inhabits eternity, whose name is Holy: "I dwell in the high and holy place, with him who has a contrite and humble spirit, to revive the spirit of the humble, and to revive the heart of the contrite ones....I have seen his ways, and will heal him."

(Isaiah 57:15, 18)

God has promised to dwell with those who have contrite hearts and humble spirits. He will reveal Himself to you and release His power and anointing in your life. You will become a channel through which He will pour out His power and glory.

WALKING IN THE SUPERNATURAL

PERSONAL APPLICATION

Those who will be greatly used in this coming move of God's Spirit will be living holy, consecrated lives. Before Christ returns for His bride, the church, He will come to purge, cleanse, and prepare her for His coming.

In your desire to walk in the supernatural, you must be willing to submit yourself to the purifying fire of the Holy Spirit, and cry out for God to purge everything in your life that is displeasing to Him.

Therefore, pursue holiness:

- Get alone with God in seasons of prayer and fasting. As you come into His presence, humble yourself and be willing to stand before Him spiritually naked—stripped of your spiritual pride.

- Submit yourself to the fire of God's Spirit. Ask the Father to reveal areas in your life where you are still struggling with carnal desires. Make the cry of your heart, "O God, consume me with Your fire! Burn out all sin and everything in my life that is offensive to You."

- Walk before God in a spirit of humility and repentance.

For thus saith the high and lofty One that inhabiteth eternity, whose name is Holy; I dwell in the high and holy place, with him also that is of a contrite and humble spirit, to revive the spirit of the humble, and to revive the heart of the contrite ones. (Isaiah 57:15)

CHAPTER NINE

GOD'S MANIFEST PRESENCE

Walking in the supernatural also means having a fresh revelation of God's glory. It is essential that you understand how God intends for you to live in an atmosphere of His glory, and for His glory to be manifested through you to the world.

Today, a deep cry is rising from a holy remnant within the body of Christ. It is resonating throughout the heavens, "Lord, show us Your glory. We want to draw near and behold You in the fullness of Your glory!"

Is this the cry and longing of your heart?

THE FULLNESS OF GOD'S DIVINE ATTRIBUTES

The Hebrew word in the Old Testament referring to God's glory is *kabowd*, meaning "honor, abundance, riches, splendor." The Greek word in the New Testament for God's glory is *doxa*, which refers to all that God is and all that God has in the fullness of His divine attributes.

In this new spiritual dimension God is bringing the church into, we will again see an awesome manifestation of His glory in our midst. As in the past, there will be times during our church services, conferences, and large gatherings where God's glory will come down in such a measure that people will fall prostrate on their faces in worship. His glory will be so strong in meetings that they will not close, but will continue nonstop for days and even weeks.

We will see widespread occurrences of God's *shekinah* or manifest glory being revealed in gatherings and meetings where true worship is ascending to the Father. Through the years, the church has experienced powerful manifestations of God's presence where His glory has come down. Yet what we are going to see before Christ's return will be on an even greater scale than any previous manifestations of His glory and will be revealed in every nation.

> God intends for His glory to be manifested through you to the world.

As long as I live, I will never forget the night God's shekinah glory came down in one of my meetings in Knoxville, Tennessee. Thinking back on that night, it is impossible for me to adequately describe the tremendous power and glory of God we experienced. It was one of the most awesome events of my life.

I had just completed a forty-day fast. I had eaten nothing and had drunk only water during the entire forty days. During the fast, incredible miracles happened in my life. The Holy Spirit directed a number of people to me who were demon-possessed, and they received their deliverance. Some were delivered even as I prayed for them by telephone! Individuals from various states called asking for deliverance, and each one of them was set free.

The night of the crusade in Knoxville was the fortieth day of my fast. The meeting was in a city auditorium where all the full gospel churches had come together. The large facility was packed with people eager to receive a miracle.

I had lost a great deal of weight and was just skin and bones. Because of my weakened condition, I remained backstage until it was time for me to preach. The pastor who introduced me warned the people, "Do not be shocked when Brother Lowery comes to minister. He is not sick; he has just concluded a forty-day fast."

When it was time for me to minister, the chairman of the crusade helped me to the platform and gave me a tall chair upon which I could lean while I preached. When I walked to the pulpit, I heard a collective gasp from the people because I appeared emaciated to them.

I began speaking, softly, since I was extremely weak. As I talked, the Spirit of God gripped the audience as I have never witnessed in my ministry. I had been speaking for only about ten minutes when suddenly the spiritual atmosphere changed and became heavy until it seemed difficult to breathe. Like the charge of an electrical current, the room was charged with the presence of God. The Holy Spirit began to wash over the congregation like an incoming tide.

A cloud of God's shekinah glory literally came down into that auditorium. Several people saw this glory cloud. What an awesome sight! The cloud of God's glory was suspended over the heads of the people. I watched as it moved from one side of the church to the other. Everywhere the cloud moved, people fell under the power of God, without anyone touching them. All over the auditorium, people were falling under God's power. Lives were radically changed and many people were healed. It was one of the most glorious sights and experiences I have ever had.

When I had ministered for a short while, I invited those who needed to be saved to stand to their feet, and hundreds of men, women, and young people leaped up to receive Christ as Savior. We prayed the sinner's prayer together and there was an immediate outburst of praise from those who had committed their lives to Christ.

I then asked those who wanted to be filled with the Spirit to stand and raise their hands.

Again, there was a tremendous response. I asked them to repeat a prayer inviting the Spirit into their lives and instructed them, "When I say, 'Be filled with the Holy Spirit,' expect Him to come in."

It happened!

Hundreds were filled with the Spirit and began to speak in tongues as the Spirit gave them the ability. At that moment, I felt led to minister to the sick, but because of my weakened condition and the vast crowd that was present, I knew I would be unable to lay hands on them. I simply asked those who needed a miracle to stand; if they were in wheelchairs or on cots, they were to place their left hands where the pains or afflictions were and to lift their right hands.

GOD'S MANIFEST PRESENCE

The service was marked by such intensity and faith that I knew God would move in a remarkable way. I prayed in a low voice, asking for God's healing presence. Suddenly, God's power swept over the audience like a wind. It was glorious. Hundreds were healed.

- People leaped from wheelchairs and off cots and began dancing and rejoicing.
- Blind eyes were opened.
- Deaf ears were unstopped.
- Heart problems, diabetes, and other conditions were immediately healed.

THE KNOWLEDGE OF GOD'S GLORY WILL FILL THE EARTH

God never intended His glory to be something intangible or inaccessible to His people. He manifested His presence to Moses and His chosen people for a purpose. He wanted them to recognize and *know* He is the almighty, miracle-working God and to love, honor, and reverence Him all the days of their lives. He wanted to reveal His power and glory so they would understand that He was with them.

> **Whenever you are in an atmosphere where God's glory is manifested, anything can happen.**

Just as God manifested His holy, awesome presence within the tabernacle and filled it with His glory until Moses and the priests were unable to stand, He desires today to fill His church with a manifestation of His power and glory. He has promised to be a *"wall of fire"* around us and *"the glory in the midst"* of us. (See Zechariah 2:5.) He desires to reveal His glory in our midst so the world will see and know He is the almighty God who is with His people to save, heal, and deliver. He has promised, *"I will fill this temple with glory.…The glory of this latter temple shall be greater than the former"* (Haggai 2:7, 9). God has planned that the knowledge of His glory will fill the earth. *"For the earth shall be filled with the knowledge of the glory of the Lord, as the waters cover the sea"* (Habakkuk 2:14).

God's power and glory in the midst of His church will be even greater than what He manifested to Moses and the children of Israel. In this realm of glory, greater and greater miracles will take place. God will be moving among His people to bring transformation in their hearts, as well as healing in their bodies and for their emotional needs.

The great revivalist Charles G. Finney related that, during one of his meetings, God's presence and glory came down in such a mighty demonstration that the entire congregation fell from their seats within a matter of moments:

> I had not spoken to them in this direct manner for more than a quarter of an hour, when all at once an awful solemnity seemed to settle down upon them. The congregation began to fall from their seats in every direction and to cry for mercy. If I had had a sword in each hand, I could not have cut them off their seats as fast as they fell. Indeed, nearly the whole congregation were either on their knees or on the floor in less than two minutes. Everyone prayed for himself who was able to speak at all.
>
> Of course, I was obliged to stop preaching, for they no longer paid any attention.[24]

Frank Bartleman, who was used mightily by God to help lead the Azusa Street Revival in 1906, described how God's glory came down in one of the meetings:

> God came so wonderfully near us that the very atmosphere of heaven seemed to surround us. Such a divine *"weight of glory"* (2 Corinthians 4:17) was upon us that we could only lie on our faces. For a long time we could hardly even remain seated. All would be on their faces on the floor, sometimes during the whole service. I was seldom able to keep from lying full-length on the floor on my face.[25]

These examples are only a glimpse into the glory that God is going to reveal in this final hour before Christ's return. Whenever you are in an atmosphere where God's glory is manifested, anything can happen. Under the cloud of His glory is everything you need...

- His manifested presence
- The very breath of life
- Salvation, healing, and deliverance
- Strength
- Supernatural provision
- Love, joy, and peace
- Anointing

"THERE IS A PLACE BESIDE ME"

Time and again, God revealed His glory to Moses and the children of Israel. He revealed His glory through the awesome miracles He performed, and in the cloud that directed and regulated their movements in the wilderness and protected them from their enemies. The ark of the covenant was another visible sign of His presence. It was there, above the mercy seat in the Holy of Holies, that the shekinah glory of God rested. God had told Moses it was there that He would manifest His presence and meet with him. As the children of Israel traveled and went out into battle, the ark of the covenant (God's presence) went before them. As long as His presence was with them, they were invincible.

> God is not far removed from us but is here, dwelling among us, to meet every need.

God's purpose in placing the ark in the midst of the people, therefore, was to give them a visible sign that He was with them. He didn't want them to worship the ark; the ark was made sacred only because His presence was there. He wanted them to live under the covering and protection of His presence. He wanted them to know that He was not a God far removed from them but was there, dwelling among them, to meet every need.

Moses and the Israelites *saw* the manifest glory of God on the top of Mt. Sinai. *"Now Mount Sinai was completely in smoke, because the LORD descended upon it in fire. Its smoke ascended like the smoke of a furnace, and the whole mountain quaked greatly"* (Exodus 19:18). During God's visitation, the mountain shook! Thunder roared and lightning crashed across the sky as God revealed His glorious presence. And they *heard* the audible voice of God speaking to them out of the midst of the fire. (See Exodus 19:16–19.)

GOD'S MANIFEST PRESENCE

Moses went up on Mt. Sinai and entered into the glory cloud of God's presence where he remained forty days and forty nights. (See Exodus 24:18.) Again, *"the sight of the glory of the LORD was like a consuming fire on the top of the mountain in the eyes of the children of Israel"* (Exodus 24:17).

After the Israelites had sinned by worshipping the golden calf, God manifested His glory at the tabernacle and talked with Moses.

> *And it came to pass, when Moses entered the tabernacle, that the pillar of cloud descended and stood at the door of the tabernacle, and the Lord talked with Moses. All the people saw the pillar of cloud standing at the tabernacle door, and all the people rose and worshiped, each man in his tent door. So the LORD spoke to Moses face to face, as a man speaks to his friend. And he would return to the camp, but his servant Joshua the son of Nun, a young man, did not depart from the tabernacle.* (Exodus 33:9–11)

Moses had repeatedly seen and experienced God's supernatural power. He had stayed up in the mountain under God's glory cloud for forty days and forty nights. He had an intimate relationship and direct access to God whereby he talked and communed with Him face-to-face. Yet Moses' great, all-consuming desire was still, *"Show me Your glory"* (Exodus 33:18).

Something had happened to Moses as he worshipped and communed with God under the glory cloud. He had experienced a divine encounter with Jehovah God that had transformed him and left a permanent mark on his life. He had also entered into a dimension of the supernatural that had broken through natural limitations, when he fasted forty days and nights without eating or drinking any water, which is impossible in the natural. (See Exodus 24:18; see also Exodus 34:28 for a second occasion of this.)

Being in the presence of God had created within him an unquenchable love and desire for an even greater revelation of God in His fullness. Once he had experienced a taste of God's glory, he could not be satisfied with anything less than a full revelation.

God responded to Moses' cry to show him His glory. He told him,

Behold, there is a place beside Me....And while My glory passes by, I will put you in a cleft of the rock and cover you with My hand until I have passed by. Then I will take away My hand and you shall see My back; but My face shall not be seen. (Exodus 33:21–23 AMP)

The Lord then descended in a cloud of His shekinah glory. He passed before Moses, as He had promised, proclaiming His mighty name. As Moses was in His awesome presence, God's glory overshadowed him and began to radiate from his face. When Moses came down from the mountain, the shekinah glory of God was still emanating strongly from his face. Aaron and the children of Israel were afraid at first to go near him because of the radiance. (See Exodus 34:29–35.)

Just as God manifested His glory to Moses and the children of Israel, He is revealing His glory to His people today. He is opening the spiritual eyes of those who are hungry for Him and are fully yielded to Him, and He is showing His glory to them. Jehovah God Almighty, the Creator of heaven and earth, is saying to His people today, "There is a place beside Me!" He longs for you to draw near to Him—into the very Holy of Holies—whereby He will reveal Himself and overshadow you with His glory.

In his book *Eternity Invading Time,* Renny McLean wrote,

Man was created to live in an atmosphere of the glory of God. Man had the distinction of possessing the DNA of God. He was God breathed. He was God inspired. He was God's being on the earth. He was created to live in and for eternity even as His Creator in His realm.[26]

The psalmist said, *"He who dwells in the secret place of the Most High shall abide under the shadow of the Almighty"* (Psalm 91:1). To live in God's presence, we must desire Him, as Moses did, with all our hearts. He must be more precious to us than life itself.

When the Israelites sinned against God and worshipped the golden calf, God told Moses that He would not go with them.

> God opens the spiritual eyes of those who are hungry for Him and are yielded to Him.

Moses cried to the Lord, *"If Your Presence does not go with me, do not carry us up from here!"* (Exodus 33:15 AMP). Moses craved God's presence and desired it as a vital necessity for himself and the Israelites. He did not want to take one step without God's presence being with them. He had received a revelation of God's power and glory, and he knew that without His presence, they would not survive or be able to stand against their enemies. Moses asked God,

For by what shall it be known that I and Your people have found favor in Your sight? Is it not in Your going with us so that we are distinguished, I and Your people, from all the other people upon the face of the earth?…I beseech You, show me Your glory. (Exodus 33:16, 18 AMP)

The one distinguishing mark that sets apart God's people from all other peoples on the face of the earth today is His glorious presence. It is not the size of our churches, our beautiful sanctuaries, or the multimillion-dollar complexes we have built. It is not the Bible schools, seminaries, or television networks we have established. It is God's power and glory in our midst.

GOD HAS CHOSEN TO MAKE US HIS HABITATION

The almighty, omnipresent God, who created the heavens and earth, and everything on the earth; who breathed the breath of life into Adam and gave life to every living creature, has *chosen* to come down and live in the midst of His people through the gift of the indwelling Holy Spirit. The God who shook the mountains and manifested His glory in flaming fire is with us and in us!

God no longer chooses to dwell in temples made with human hands. His presence does not inhabit and remain in buildings or certain edifices. *We, His people,* are the temple where His divine presence dwells. *"For you are the temple of the living God. As God has said: 'I will dwell in them and walk among them. I will be their God, and they shall be My people'"* (2 Corinthians 6:16).

God chooses to manifest His presence and glory to the world through His people, through His sons and daughters. As we discussed in the previous chapter, when He manifests His presence, it is through yielded, clean vessels. We know what the Scriptures teach, but there are very few Christians who have had a real revelation deep within their spirits where they recognize that the presence of the almighty, miracle-working God is living *within* them.

Most Christians have a concept of God as being far removed somewhere in the heavens, who may manifest His presence when the congregation assembles together for worship or during times of prayer. Yet, it is sad, but true, that God's glory is no longer evident within many churches. The people go through the motions, sing worship songs, and listen to the sermon, but they never really experience God's presence. According to George Barna, among the seventy-seven million American adults who call themselves churched, born-again Christians, "Half of all believers say they do not feel they have entered into the presence of God or experienced a genuine connection with Him during the past year."[27]

> The almighty God has *chosen* to come down and live in the midst of His people through the gift of the indwelling Holy Spirit.

Because of people's spiritual neglect and indifference toward God's presence, His Spirit is no longer moving within many churches. His presence has been replaced by tradition, rigid schedules, and man-made programs. People come week after week but remain untouched and unchanged by God's power.

Many Christians, including pastors and ministers, have become self-righteous and dependent on their own natural abilities, so they no longer have a deep, earnest desire to seek God and His presence. Others have reached a point of false contentment in their spiritual growth where they no longer feel a great need to diligently seek God, wait before Him in His presence, draw upon His strength, and receive His direction. Instead, they rely on their own spiritual "reserve" until the anointing, which comes from being in God's presence, is no longer there.

DEVELOP TOTAL DEPENDENCE
UPON GOD'S PRESENCE

You must develop a total dependence upon God's presence and learn to live under the cloud of His glory, not letting anything cause you to come out from under it. Let it be over you, under you, ahead of you, and following you. Be enveloped and consumed by it. If the presence of God is not with you in what you are doing, turn back and find Him. If His presence has gone ahead of you, and you have not realized it, rise up and *run after Him.*

It is easy to get so busy, even in our work for the Lord, that we don't have time to notice that the glory of God's presence has moved and we are being left behind. We must learn to develop a spiritual sensitivity to God's glory. Then, when the cloud of His glory starts to move, we can rise up and quickly follow it.

God wants to bring you into a new position of strength that comes from living in the presence of His glory. As you learn to live and walk continually in His presence, you will become fearless.

GOD'S MANIFEST PRESENCE

- When pain or sickness comes, you will not be afraid.

- When you face a financial crisis—when the bank is ready to foreclose on your house or you don't have enough money to pay your bills—you will not be fearful or moved by your circumstances.

- When you experience a crisis in your family in which the enemy is trying to tear your family apart or destroy your marriage, you will not panic or give up because of what you see in the natural.

When you learn to live under the cloud of God's presence, you will not be moved regardless of what trials or circumstances you may face.

It doesn't matter what you may *feel*. God's presence in your life isn't based upon whether or not you feel His presence. You may walk through dark valleys where it will seem as if absolutely no one understands and there is no one to turn to who really cares. But, regardless of how you may feel, when you are living and walking in an awareness of His glorious presence, you will stand firm.

King David, who was a great warrior, knew God's presence was continually with him. He said, *"I have set the LORD always before me; because He is at my right hand I shall not be moved"* (Psalm 16:8). David made it a priority to set his heart and mind upon God. He had determined—he had set his spiritual focus—to keep the Lord always before him, recognizing His presence in every circumstance he faced.

Too often, we forget that God's presence is with us, and so we complain, worry, and fall to pieces. It will take a conscious act on your part to be sensitive to His presence and to determine that you will not take one step or do one thing unless His glory, power, and anointing are with you. Your highest priority and the greatest desire of your heart must be, "Lord, show me Your glory!" David said, *"**One thing I have desired of the Lord,** that will I seek: that I may dwell in the house of the Lord all the days of my life, to behold the beauty of the Lord, and to inquire in His temple"* (Psalm 27:4, emphasis added). David's desire wasn't set upon acquiring wealth, obtaining the favor of men, or building his kingdom. He longed to live continually in God's presence.

> **God wants to bring you into a new position of strength that comes from living in the presence of His glory.**

What about you? Do you want a fresh manifestation of God's power and presence? Then you must earnestly seek to have a full revelation of His glory. You must hunger and thirst for Him with all that is in you. To walk in the glory and supernatural power of God, you must wait before Him, commune and fellowship with Him, and draw upon His strength so that you are constantly renewed and refreshed by Him. If you want to live continually under the cloud of God's glory, ask yourself...

- Am I earnestly and diligently seeking God?
- Do I really hunger and thirst for His presence?
- Do I set aside time to wait in God's presence, spend time in prayer, be in His Word, and praise and worship Him?

- Have I become too complacent, busy, and involved with my personal desires that I no longer take time to stay in God's presence until His power and glory are manifested in my life?

GOD DESIRES TO REVEAL HIS GLORY IN YOU

This is the hour when God has planned for His glory to be especially seen upon His people. It is the time when the *"earth will be filled with the knowledge of the glory of the* LORD, *as the waters cover the sea"* (Habakkuk 2:14). How will this be possible? Through a *holy* remnant that will be a living demonstration and manifestation of His glory and power. God's purpose through Christ's death and resurrection was not only to save and redeem us from our sins, but also to bring *"many sons unto glory."*

> *But we see Jesus, who was made a little lower than the angels, for the suffering of death crowned with glory and honor, that He, by the grace of God, might taste death for everyone. For it was fitting for Him, for whom are all things and by whom are all things, in bringing many sons to glory, to make the captain of their salvation perfect through sufferings.* (Hebrews 2:9–10)

In the Father-heart of God, there is a desire to have many sons and daughters who possess and reflect His glory. What this means is that God has called you to manifest Christ's glory through your relationship with Him. The apostle Paul said, *"[It was] to this end that He called you through our Gospel, so that you may obtain and share in the glory of our Lord Jesus Christ (the Messiah)"* (2 Thessalonians 2:14 AMP).

God intends for you not only to know the unspeakable riches of His glory, but also to *obtain* them. You are called to obtain His glory! The key to obtaining the riches of God's glory is summed up in Colossians 1:27: *"To them God willed to make known what are the riches of the glory of this mystery among the Gentiles: which is **Christ in you, the hope of glory**"* (emphasis added). The key is Christ in you.

Paul said God was pleased to reveal to us the greatness of the riches of His glory. He told the believers in Rome, *"That He might make known the riches of His glory on the vessels of mercy, which He had prepared beforehand for glory, even us whom He called, not of the Jews only, but also of the Gentiles"* (Romans 9:23–24). His glory is not something beyond your reach. It is not something intangible. The Father intends all His sons and daughters to possess it. It is part of your spiritual inheritance.

JESUS WAS A FULL MANIFESTATION OF GOD'S GLORY

To understand how God's glory is to be revealed *in* us and *through* us, we must understand how His glory was manifested through Christ. God prophesied through Isaiah that He would reveal His glory to the world: *"The glory of the LORD shall be revealed, and all flesh shall see it together; for the mouth of the LORD has spoken"* (Isaiah 40:5). This promise was fulfilled when Christ came to earth. He was a full revelation of the Father's glory. His life, words, and actions were manifestations of God's glory. *"And the Word became flesh and dwelt among us, and we beheld His glory, the glory as of the only begotten of the Father, full of grace and truth"* (John 1:14).

Though Jesus was born of a woman and lived His life on earth as a human being, He was the divine and eternal Son of God. The writer of the book of Hebrews described Jesus as *"the brightness of* [God's] *glory and the express image of his person"* (Hebrews 1:3). The word *"glory"* in this verse is again translated from the Greek word *doxa,* which refers to all that God has and is—the totality of His being. In the form of human flesh, Jesus was a demonstration of God's glory. The glory of God shone forth and was manifested both in Jesus' character and His actions.

The world saw the awesome glory of God in the person of Jesus! As He lived and walked among people, He revealed God's glory—His great love, mercy, forgiveness, longsuffering, and kindness. He made known God's glory as He healed the sick, cast out demons, and set the oppressed free. In writing to the Colossians, Paul described Jesus as being *"the image of the invisible God, the firstborn over all creation"* (Colossians 1:15). In this verse, the word *"image"* points to Christ as being the *visible representation and manifestation of God.* While Jesus lived His life on this earth as the Son of God, He was the *exact image of God*—the visible representation and manifestation of God to men.

> **God intends for you not only to know the unspeakable riches of His glory, but also to *obtain* them.**

Jesus said, *"He who sees Me sees Him who sent Me"* (John 12:45). Likewise, when Philip asked Jesus, *"Show us the Father"* (John 14:8), Jesus answered, *"Have I been with you so long, and yet you have not known Me, Philip?* **He who has seen Me has seen the Father;** *so how can you say, 'Show us the Father'?"* (John 14:9, emphasis added). It was difficult for Philip and the other disciples to fully understand how a Man with whom they walked, talked, and lived could be God. When they looked at Jesus, they saw someone who got tired, hungry, and sleepy, just as they did. They did not comprehend who Jesus really was until after His resurrection. Yet when Jesus told Philip, *"He who has seen Me has seen the Father,"* He was referring to the life of God proceeding from His innermost being. The glory, life, and fullness of the Father were revealed through Him.

Peter, James, and John were privileged to actually see an outward physical manifestation of God's glory radiating from Jesus' body. Jesus had taken them up to the mountain with Him to pray. While He prayed, God's glory began to be revealed in Him. His face shone as bright as the sun, and even His clothes pulsated with light. (See Matthew 17:1–6.)

Right before the disciples' eyes, Jesus was transfigured. The word *"transfigured"* (Matthew 17:2) used in this passage is translated from the Greek word *metamorphoo*, signifying a change. It is taken from the root word *morphi*, which refers to "an outward expression which proceeds from and is representative of one's inward character." When Jesus was transfigured before His disciples, the glory of God that proceeded from and was representative of His inward character began to shine forth.

CHRIST IN YOU, THE HOPE OF GLORY!

You are destined to obtain Christ's glory. I am not talking about the glory that will be revealed in us at Christ's appearing. (See Colossians 3:4.) God has purposed to reveal His glory *to you* and *through you* today. Jesus Christ, in the form of a man, was the *"express image"* (Hebrews 1:3) of God. He reflected His Father's glory—all that the Father has and is. Likewise, God has planned for us, in the form of human flesh, to be the "image" of our Elder Brother, Jesus Christ, who dwells within us. *"For whom* [God] *foreknew, He also predestined to be conformed to the image of His Son, that He might be the firstborn among many brethren"* (Romans 8:29). We are to reflect Christ's glory through our words and actions as an outward testimony to the world.

The word *"image"* in Romans 8:29 is translated from the Greek word *eikon,* which refers to believers being a representation of who God is. It does not mean merely *resembling* Christ, but *representing* Him. You are to represent *Him,* not an imitation or something like Him, but what He is in His glory.

> **The key to being changed and conformed into Christ's image is your *union* with Him.**

Consider for a moment the glory that is in Christ, who is seated in a position of supreme power and authority at the right hand of God the Father. (See, for example, Hebrews 1:3.) The fullness of God is in Him: *"God was pleased to have all his fullness dwell in him"* (Colossians 1:19 NIV). The apostle Paul said that the fullness of God dwells in Christ, and through our union with Him, we partake in this fullness. (See Colossians 2:9–10 NIV.)

Let this great truth sink deep into your spirit. If Christ is in you, you are also filled with the fullness of the Godhead—Father, Son, and Holy Spirit. This is the glory He has planned to be revealed and manifested through your life. The key to being changed and conformed into Christ's image, with His glory being manifested in and through your life, is your *union* with Him. Jesus said, *"If you abide in Me, and My words abide in you, you will ask what you desire, and it shall be done for you"* (John 15:7).

The key is Christ in you, the hope of glory!

You must remain in Christ—vitally united to Him through continual communion and a living relationship. In Him, you have the very life-flow of God, in all His power and glory, manifested within you. You are a partaker of His divine nature. (See 2 Peter 1:4.) *"We, who with unveiled faces all reflect the Lord's glory, are being transformed into his likeness with ever-increasing glory, which comes from the Lord, who is the Spirit"* (2 Corinthians 3:18 NIV).

From the beginning, it has been God's intention that His sons and daughters not only live in His glory, but also *manifest* His glory to the world. His purpose for your life is that, through your relationship with Christ, you will be transformed into His image and likeness, and His supernatural power and glory will be manifested through you to heal the sick, cast out demons, raise the dead, and do the same works Jesus did when He was on earth.

SIX KEYS TO WALKING IN GOD'S GLORY

At His appointed time, God supernaturally gave the church birth. He called forth a people and breathed the Holy Spirit upon them. He anointed them with His unlimited authority and power and commissioned them. Now, at His appointed time, He is bringing His church into a new position of full maturity whereby His people are taking their positions as full-grown sons and daughters and joint-heirs of His kingdom. God is releasing an end-time anointing because He desires that His power and glory be manifested through us, and He wants us to be filled with His fullness. The following are six keys that will help you to walk in God's glory.

1. RECOGNIZE THAT YOU ARE CALLED TO OBTAIN HIS GLORY

"He called you by our gospel, for the obtaining of the glory of our Lord Jesus Christ" (2 Thessalonians 2:14). You may look at your weaknesses, failures, and limitations, and think it is impossible for you to be changed into Christ's image, where His glory is manifested through your life. Not only is it possible, but the Father has also made full provision for it. God purposed that we should grow into *"the measure of the stature of the fullness of Christ"* (Ephesians 4:13). By His Spirit within you, He is working to bring you to a point where you are spiritually complete, having the stature of the fullness of Jesus.

This divine purpose is not something to overlook or reject simply because you may not understand it or feel it is possible. The power to conform you into Christ's image where His glory is manifested in and through you is in the incorruptible seed God has placed within you. Christ's life grows and develops in you as you nourish that life and are fully yielded to the Holy Spirit.

By faith, begin to act upon what God has revealed to you through the Scriptures. Feed on the "strong meat" of the Word and apply it in your life so that you are walking in obedience to Christ. (See Hebrews 5:13–14.)

2. MAKE YOUR HEART'S CRY, "LORD, SHOW ME YOUR GLORY!"

A manifestation of God's power and presence will not somehow fall from the heavens upon you. Don't go from one meeting to another looking for His presence and glory. God doesn't make His habitation in buildings. *"Do you not know that you are the temple of God and that the Spirit of God dwells in you?"* (1 Corinthians 3:16). God's presence and glory will be manifested within sanctified vessels, within men and women who have yielded themselves *fully* to Him.

As we saw, God has promised, *"I will fill this temple with glory.…* *The glory of this latter temple shall be greater than the former"* (Haggai 2:7, 9). The body of Christ is the *"latter temple."* Before Christ returns for His church, He will come to manifest His power and glory within those who are hungering for Him—who are waiting, longing, and expecting Him to manifest Himself to them.

Again, don't limit God or try to make Him fit within your preconceived ideas of how, when, or where you think He will manifest Himself to you. Through the indwelling of God's Spirit, you have become the *habitation* of God where His presence dwells. (See Ephesians 2:22 KJV.) As you place your total dependence upon Him, He will manifest His glory, power, and presence in your life.

3. UNDERSTAND CHRIST HAS GIVEN HIS GLORY TO HIS CHURCH

Before He went to the cross, Jesus prayed to the Father for His church,

And the glory which You gave Me I have given them, that they may be one just as We are one: I in them, and You

in Me; that they may be made perfect in one, and that the world may know that You have sent Me, and have loved them as You have loved Me. (John 17:22–23)

In this prayer, Jesus was not just talking about the unity of the church. He prayed that you and I would enter into the close union of God the Father in Christ, and Christ in us—where we would be one in *Them. "I in them, and You in Me; that they may be made perfect in one."*

Jesus made it very clear that He has given His church—you and me—the *same* glory He had with the Father. Since Christ has given you His glory, He now wants you to walk in it and allow His glory to be revealed in and through you. How does this happen?

We know that Jesus' words, actions, and works were all a result of the Father living in Him. He said,

The words that I speak to you I do not speak on My own authority; but the Father who dwells in Me does the works. (John 14:10)

The Son can do nothing of Himself, but what He sees the Father do; for whatever He does, the Son also does in like manner. (John 5:19)

I do nothing of Myself; but as My Father taught Me, I speak these things. (John 8:28)

The Father is in Me, and I in Him. (John 10:38)

Once more, we see the significance of our unity with Christ. Both Jesus and the Father live within us. Jesus said, *"If anyone loves Me, he will keep My word; and My Father will love him, and We will come to him and make Our home with him"* (John 14:23). It is in this union—God the Father dwelling in Christ, Christ the Son of God dwelling in you—that you will be able to reflect God's glory and do the same works Jesus did. Jesus said, *"If I do not do the works of My Father, do not believe Me; but if I do, though you do not believe Me, believe the works, that you may know and believe that the Father is in Me, and I in Him"* (John 10:37–38). You must have the same type of relationship in which you know—not just think or wish—but *know* Christ is in you doing His work through you, revealing His power and glory.

4. YIELD YOURSELF FULLY TO THE HOLY SPIRIT WORKING IN YOU

Again, you are not changed into something that *looks* like Christ, but into the *"same image from glory to glory, just as by the Spirit of the Lord"* (2 Corinthians 3:18, emphasis added). It may still be hard for you to grasp how you, with all your human limitations, can be changed into Christ's image whereby God's glory and power is flowing out of you as it flowed out of Jesus—healing the sick, opening blind eyes, causing the lame to walk, casting out demons, and setting people free from all types of sickness and disease. Yet this transformation into Christ's image is accomplished by His Spirit living in you.

> **If we truly desire to walk in God's glory, we must make preparation for it in every area of our lives.**

Remember that His Spirit does not *compel* you to think, act, talk, and live as Jesus did. He works in your life to the extent that you *yield* to Him. You must make a deliberate choice.

You must not only desire it, but you must also actively seek it. As we have learned, this transformation into Christ's image must first take place in your mind: *"Do not be conformed to this world, but be transformed by the renewing of your mind"* (Romans 12:2). This transformation takes place as the Word of God truly abides in you. I'm not talking about just *reading* the Word or *hearing* the Word. The Word must penetrate your mind and spirit. You have to continually meditate on it, day and night, so it does not depart from your mind.

As the Word takes root in your spirit, your mind will be renewed. Your spiritual eyes will open, and you will be able to see Christ clearly. You will begin to know God's will and see all the things God has prepared for you. Then, as you yield yourself to His Spirit working in you, His power and glory will be released in your life.

5. PRESENT YOURSELF AS A VESSEL OF WORSHIP

Worship is essential to entering into God's presence and the realm of His glory. It is in this realm that we are able to take hold of His supernatural power and the miracles we need.

This is the day of God's glory. If we truly desire to walk in that glory, we must make preparation for it in every area of our lives. For example, we must make room for God's glory in our church services and conferences. The major reason why God's glory is not being manifested in the churches across our nation and around the world is that we haven't allowed Him to work. Instead of having our services completely programmed, we must allow time for God's Spirit to move, for Him to speak to us, and for Him to minister healing and deliverance.

We need God to so move on our hearts that we enter a new dimension of worship. He is looking for those who will worship Him in Spirit and truth. (See John 4:23–24.) So much of the worship in our churches is entertainment-oriented rather than focused on leading people into God's presence. The majority of Christians sitting in our pews have not had a revelation of what genuine worship really is.

True worship is much more than just singing songs. It involves acknowledging God and lifting our hearts to Him as we reverence Him for who He is. It is about pleasing God and pouring out our love upon Him. We must abandon ourselves to Him—forgetting everything else and honoring Him with all that we are and have. There may be times when God moves upon us to dance before Him, as David did, with all our hearts. We may feel led to sing a new song in the Spirit, to weep, to fall prostrate on our faces, or just to wait in silence for Him to speak to us. True worship such as this brings us into the very throne room of God. In response, God's presence and glory comes down in our midst. The key is being willing to make room for God to do in us whatever He wants.

In your personal life, make room for God to manifest His glory. Make time in your schedule to just worship Him. Don't ask Him for anything, but minister to Him and pour out your love upon Him. Set aside quality time daily to wait before Him in earnest expectation for His presence to come and overshadow you as the glory cloud overshadowed Moses.

6. DEVELOP AN INTIMATE KNOWLEDGE OF CHRIST

Similarly, you must come into a deep, intimate knowledge of Christ. Just as Jesus was able to say of the Father, "*I know Him, for I am from Him, and He sent Me"* (John 7:29), you must be able to say, "I know Christ because I am from Him." To truly know Christ and reflect His glory, you must make it a top priority to spend time in His presence, diligently seeking Him with your whole heart. Read His words in the Scriptures and meditate on them. You must set your desire upon Him, and *wait* before Him, recognizing your total dependence upon Him for guidance, strength, anointing, and the meeting of all your needs. You must say, as John the Baptist did, *"He must increase, but I must decrease"* (John 3:30).

OVERSHADOWED WITH HIS GLORY

Just as God called Moses up to the mount where the cloud of His glory covered him, He is calling you to enter into a relationship with Him where the glory of His presence overshadows you.

As you wait in His presence, you will begin to walk in His strength and power. His life will flow into you, and His glory will be manifested through you. God's desire to reveal His glory within the church today is far greater than your desire to come into a place where you are spiritually positioned to *experience* His power and glory.

Remember the above steps to walking in God's glory, and begin to apply them in your life. In response to Moses' cry, *"Show me Your glory"* (Exodus 33:18), God responded, *"There is a place beside Me"* (v. 21 AMP). The Father is saying to you this very moment, "My beloved child, there is a place beside Me. Come up into the mountain and meet with Me. I will enfold you in My glory. I am longing for you. I have set My love and desire upon you, and I am waiting for you."

In the next chapter, we will see that the Father is calling His sons and daughters to go beyond the veil into the Holy of Holies where He has given us *unlimited access* to His presence. You will discover more about how to develop an intimate relationship with Him, where you are communing with God face-to-face; where the incense of your love, worship, and intercession is offered in power, and where the rivers of living water are flowing forth into your life.

GOD'S MANIFEST PRESENCE

PERSONAL APPLICATION

One of the major steps you must take to walk in God's glory is to present yourself as a vessel of worship. The Father is looking for *"true worshippers"* and is waiting to release His miracle power on their behalf.

> *The hour is coming, and now is, when the true worshippers will worship the Father in spirit and truth; for the Father is seeking such to worship Him. God is Spirit, and those who worship Him must worship in spirit and truth.* (John 4:23–24)

> *For the eyes of the LORD run to and fro throughout the whole earth, to show Himself strong on behalf of those whose heart is loyal to Him.*
> (2 Chronicles 16:9)

Remember that true worship is acknowledging God for who He is. It is not about us. It is all about Him. It is about pleasing Him and pouring out our love upon Him.

Especially apply steps 5 and 6 from this chapter. During your personal time with the Lord, make it a top priority to make room for Him to manifest His glory. Wait upon the Lord—not asking Him for anything, but just worshipping Him. Minister to Him by exalting and lifting up His name. Wait quietly in His presence, silently adoring Him, honoring His great love, faithfulness, mercy, patience, kindness, and all His divine attributes.

Daily wait upon Him and earnestly expect His presence to come and overshadow you. In response to your worship, He will manifest His presence. Draw close to Him and allow Him to reveal His heart to you.

The key is your willingness to make room for God to manifest His power in your life in whatever manner He chooses.

CHAPTER TEN

LIVING IN THE HOLIEST

We are the generation that will witness the greatest manifestations of God's power and glory ever seen. Not only will we see it with our eyes, but those who are walking in *intimate relationship* with God will also be channels through which His supernatural power will be released.

We have learned that a deep relationship with God is fundamental to having His miracle power flowing through our lives. If you desire to walk in the supernatural, there is no substitute for this. You must develop a relationship with the Lord in which He is your first love—above even your spouse, your children, your ministry, and your career. You must have an unquenchable desire to *know* Him in His fullness. Just as the apostle Paul cried out, *"That I may know Him and the power of His resurrection"* (Philippians 3:10), this must be the greatest desire of your heart.

Moses, Elijah, Elisha, David, Daniel, Peter, Paul, Philip, and all those recorded in the Word who not only witnessed mighty manifestations of God's miracle power, but also were used by God in manifesting them, had one thing in common—their intimate relationship with God Almighty.

WALKING IN THE SUPERNATURAL

We have received a royal summons from the throne room of God. Proceeding forth from His very heart, and heralded by the Holy Spirit, the cry is heard, "Draw near to Me. Enter into the Holiest and commune with Me as a beloved child with His Father. I want you to know and love Me with all that is within you."

We have been granted unlimited access into the awesome presence of God. Jesus paid the ultimate price so that the veil separating man from God has been forever severed. By His own blood, He opened the way for us to come boldly and enter the Holiest. (See Hebrews 10:19.) Yet a great majority of Christians are unwilling to come into God's presence to know Him intimately. They relegate a minimal amount of time to real, life-changing communion and fellowship with God. How the heart of Father God must be grieved as His call goes un-heeded. Millions claiming to know Him are content with what is infinitely inferior, substituting…

- works for relationship.
- religious rituals for true worship.
- sacrifice for obedience.
- tradition for intimacy.

GOD DESIRES COVENANT RELATIONSHIP

Throughout the ages, God has chosen to enter into *covenant relationship* with His people. On Mt. Sinai, when He came down to meet with Moses and the Israelites, the people saw the awesome manifestation of His glory, and they heard His audible voice, but instead of reverencing Him, they trembled in fear. Their fear became a barrier that separated them from

God's manifest presence and prevented them from having intimate communion with Him, even though Moses encouraged them not to be afraid of the Lord. They sent the heads of their tribes to Moses, saying, in effect, "If we hear God's voice any more, we will die! You go near and hear what He is saying. Then, come and tell us what He has said and we will do it." (See Exodus 20:18–21.)

Like the children of Israel, many believers today are afraid or unwilling to pay the price to develop an intimate relationship with the Lord in which they can know Him for themselves. They are unwilling to go beyond the veil into the Holy of Holies. They do not desire to break through the barriers separating them from true intimacy with the Lord. Instead, they are satisfied to remain at their current level,

> **Walking in the supernatural involves continual communion with God as you listen for His voice and follow His direction.**

where they depend solely upon others to interpret the Word for them and reveal to them what God is saying. They are not in a position to know and hear His voice for themselves. Walking in the supernatural, however, involves continual communion with God where you are listening for His voice and being led and directed by Him. This communion with Him should be a normal occurrence in your life, not an exception.

God is calling His sons and daughters to forsake their fear and complacency and to go beyond the veil into the Holiest. The Father wants a 24/7 relationship with us. He doesn't want us to just commune with Him and hear His voice sporadically but to live in intimate communion with Him on a day-to-day basis. The more time you spend in the presence of God, the more you will be ready for Him to take you into this supernatural dimension of His power.

It is in God's presence that we are changed and His power and anointing are released to flow through us. To walk in the supernatural, you must go beyond what you have learned *about* God and His power through your natural understanding, into a *revelation* of who He is. This type of relationship does not develop simply by being in church every time the doors are open. It does not merely develop through a regimented study of the Word. You must spend time in God's holy presence—communing with Him and loving and worshipping Him with all that is in you.

We don't have to tremble in fear at the sound of His voice. We have been brought into the kingdom of God as His sons and daughters. We can now go boldly into His presence crying, *"Abba, Father"* (Romans 8:15).

For you have not come to the mountain that may be touched and that burned with fire, and to blackness and darkness and tempest, and the sound of a trumpet and the voice of words, so that those who heard it begged that the word should not be spoken to them anymore....But you have come to Mount Zion and to the city of the living God, the heavenly Jerusalem, to an innumerable company of angels, to the general assembly and church of the firstborn who are registered in heaven, to God the Judge of all, to the spirits of just men made perfect, to Jesus the Mediator of the new

covenant, and to the blood of sprinkling that speaks better
things than that of Abel. (Hebrews 12:18–19, 22–24)

We have come to Mount Zion, the city of the living God, through His Son Jesus Christ.

GOD HAS ALWAYS DESIRED TO MANIFEST HIMSELF TO HIS PEOPLE

From the very beginning, God has always taken great pleasure in manifesting Himself in a tangible way to His people. As He walked with Adam in the cool of the evening (see Genesis 3:8), He desires to walk and fellowship with us. He wants us to become a people who will live in His manifest presence.

Merriam-Webster's 11th Collegiate Dictionary defines *manifest* as "readily perceived by the senses; easily understood or recognized by the mind; obvious." This is the way God desires to make Himself known to His people in these final days before Christ's return. While we have read about His visitations in church history and even witnessed them, we should realize that God never intended to just *visit* His people. He has always desired a people in whom His presence would permanently live.

We serve an awesome God who wants to make Himself known and to communicate with His children. He is calling us to a place of deep relationship where we can commune on a regular basis, where He can speak to us and share His innermost desires. He wants to reveal His heart, plans, and purposes to us, and He desires to release His life into us.

The great Christian leader A. W. Tozer once said that God "waits to show Himself in ravishing fullness to the humble of soul and the pure in heart."[28] This will happen as soon as there is a church waiting to have Him revealed in ravishing fullness. God is longing for a people who will hunger for His presence and will be willing to give up everything, if necessary, to receive it. He is searching for a people who will cry out, "Lord, come manifest Yourself in my life. Break through every limitation of my natural desires, theology, traditions, preconceived ideas, and everything else that stands in the way of my experiencing the fullness of Your presence. Change me. Do whatever You need to do in my life. I give myself fully to You."

Is this the cry of your heart?

We have seen that God directed Moses to build a tabernacle where He would meet with him and the children of Israel. The tabernacle building and its outer court, as well as its furnishings, were built at God's direction and according to His pattern. It was a representation of His presence and a shadow of the heavenly sanctuary.

> **In God's presence we are changed, and His power and anointing are released to flow through us.**

Let us take a close look at the pattern God established for the tabernacle, so we can understand more clearly His desire and plan to bring His sons and daughters into a personal, vibrant relationship with Him, where He can live and remain in them.

Every part of the tabernacle, with its various furnishings, is filled with deep spiritual significance. It is not my desire to give you an intensive study of the tabernacle. I want to draw, from its rich symbolism and meaning, revelation truths concerning the depths of the personal relationship God desires to bring us into today.

Are you ready to move into the Holiest, where you are breathing, talking, and living in His manifest presence?

GOD'S PATTERN FOR MEETING: THE TABERNACLE

The structure of the tabernacle building (which consisted of two rooms, the Holy Place and the Holy of Holies) was made of acacia wood, over which was its "tent" or roof, made primarily of animal skins. The Hebrew word referring to the tabernacle building itself is *mishkan,* which means "dwelling place." The word referring to the roof of the tabernacle is *ohel,* which is variously translated as *tabernacle* or *tent.* (See, for example, Exodus 27:21 KJV; Exodus 39:32 KJV, NKJV.)[29]

The Holy Place and the Holy of Holies, also known as the Holiest, were separated by a veil. Inside the Holy Place were the brass lampstand, the table of showbread, and the altar of incense. Inside the Holiest was the ark of the covenant, where God's presence dwelled between the figures of the cherubim on the ark's cover, which formed what was known as the mercy seat.

The tabernacle building was surrounded by an outer court, which featured a laver of bronze, located closest to the tabernacle building, and an altar of burnt offering, which was near the entrance to the court.

Working from the outside in, there was therefore...

- The Outer Court
- The Holy Place
- The Holiest or Holy of Holies

As we review these three areas of the tabernacle, ask the Holy Spirit to reveal to you the depths of the intimate relationship the Father desires to have with you.

THE OUTER COURT

The outer court was the place where the people came to offer sacrifices and burnt offerings to God. The priests were required to wash in the bronze laver before approaching God and offering the sacrifices on the altar. God instructed Moses, *"A fire shall always be burning on the altar; it shall never go out"* (Leviticus 6:13). This fire was to be a continual reminder that God's presence was with them.

Anyone could enter the outer court, but was separated from the Holy Place and the Holiest. This clearly revealed the separation between God and man because of man's sinful state. This fact was reinforced by the curtain on the door of the Holy Place and the veil that closed off the Holy of Holies.

The burnt sacrifices on the altar signified that only through the sacrifice and shedding of blood could humanity be reconciled to God. While the blood of animals and the washing by water served as a means of temporarily purifying and cleansing, these were figures or types of Christ, who was to come, shed His blood, and provide the perfect sacrifice and cleansing for our sins.

> *Not with the blood of goats and calves, but with His own blood He entered the Most Holy Place once for all, having obtained eternal redemption.* (Hebrews 9:12)

Many Christians have an outer-court relationship with God. Through the blood of Jesus, they have received forgiveness of their sins and have been given free and unlimited access into the Holiest, where God's presence dwells. The veil separating them from the fullness of His presence has been removed, but they never venture into even the Holy Place. They remain content where they are—satisfied that their sins are forgiven, without much thought to having a deepening relationship with their heavenly Father.

Christians in the outer court attend church, sing, pray, and go through the motions. But they have a Sunday-morning, once-a-week relationship with God. They have no real communion and fellowship with Him on a daily basis. When they were first saved, their hearts may have burned with passion for the Lord, but the fire has gone out. They do not hunger to grow closer in communion and fellowship with Him. They have become lukewarm and halfhearted, *"having a form of godliness but denying its power"* (2 Timothy 3:5). They are unwilling to pay the price to live in the Holiest where God's glory and presence dwell.

Yet, through Christ, the invitation has gone out, *"Therefore, brethren, having boldness to enter the Holiest by the blood of Jesus,…let us draw near"* (Hebrews 10:19, 22).

THE HOLY PLACE

Only the priests who had been sanctified and set apart were allowed to enter the Holy Place of the tabernacle. Inside was the golden lampstand, the table of showbread, and the altar of incense. The light in the lampstand was never to go out.

Aaron and selected priests went into the Holy Place, where they ministered to God before the altar of incense. They ate of the showbread and offered up incense before Him continually, day and night. The altar of incense was at the very heart of the tabernacle; it was closest to the veil separating the Holy Place from the Holiest.

When the priests offered up the incense, the Holy Place was filled with smoke and with the sweet-smelling perfume of the incense. The incense symbolized the intercession and worship of God's people arising to Him. (Compare Revelation 5:8; 8:3.) Its continual burning represented unbroken fellowship with God.

> **Christ opened the way for us not only to enter the Holiest, but also to *live* and *remain* in God's presence.**

There are Christians who have lifted the curtain from the outer court and entered the Holy Place. They have taken their position at the altar as priests unto God. (See 1 Peter 2:9; Revelation 5:10.) They have tasted of God's glory, but they have not yet developed the kind of relationship where they are continually living in the fullness of His presence.

Christians living in the Holy Place are very involved in serving God, working in the church, and ministering to the needs of others. They read their Bibles, pray, and are focused on doing things *for* the Lord, but they are not ministering *to* the Lord by offering themselves as living sacrifices to Him.

Those who remain in the Holy Place, but fail to enter into the Holiest, have not yet had a revelation concerning the intimate relationship the Father desires His children to have with Him. They have heard the call. They know Christ has opened up the way, and they are hungry to know the Lord in His power and glory. But they have not persevered enough to break through the barriers preventing them from going into the Holiest. They still have not died to self and all that draws them away from this deepest relationship with the Father. Yet, again, the invitation has been given, *"Therefore, brethren, having boldness to enter the Holiest by the blood of Jesus,…let us draw near"* (Hebrews 10:19, 22).

THE HOLIEST

For approximately fifteen centuries, Israel had a sanctuary (first the tabernacle, then the temple) with a Holiest place, into which no one might enter except for the high priest, once a year. The penalty for anyone else entering was death! On the Day of Atonement, the high priest was allowed to go beyond the veil, enter the Holiest, and sprinkle the blood from the sacrifice onto the mercy seat of the ark of the covenant.

In the tabernacle, the Holiest measured fifteen feet high, fifteen feet wide, and fifteen feet long. The ark of the covenant was where God's presence was manifested. The Lord told Moses, *"And there I will meet with you, and I will speak with you from above the mercy seat, from between the two cherubim which are on the ark of the Testimony* [covenant]" (Exodus 25:22).

Again, the ark was carried before the children of Israel by the priests as they traveled, and was placed in the Holiest in the tabernacle when they rested. God wanted the people to be constantly reminded that He was with them. He wanted them to know that He was not a God far removed from them, but that He was there, dwelling among them, to meet every need.

For hundreds of years, therefore, the Israelites saw various manifestations of God's presence but were shut out from the Holiest and were unable to have intimate fellowship with Him. Then, at God's appointed time, Christ offered Himself once as the one perfect Sacrifice to cleanse human beings from their sins. When He cried on the cross, *"It is finished!"* (John 19:30), the veil separating humanity from the Holiest was torn in two, from top to bottom. (See, for example, Matthew 27:50–51.) Jesus opened the way for us into the Holiest!

Christ entered the Holiest through the tearing of His own flesh, represented by the veil, and through His blood has opened the way for us not only to enter the Holiest, but also to *live* and *remain* in God's presence.

You were meant to live in God's presence. The Spirit of God is calling you to enter the Holiest, into the place where God's presence dwells, where Christ, your Great High Priest lives, to live and work always in the presence of your Father.

The Holiest is the place of God's manifest presence…

- Where you are able to commune with Him directly.
- Where His holiness is revealed and you are made holy in Him.
- Where the incense of love, worship, and intercession is offered in power.
- Where the rivers of living water pour forth into your life.
- Where God's anointing is continuously released to flow through you.

Once more, the call goes forth,

LIVING IN THE HOLIEST

Therefore, brethren, having boldness to enter the Holiest by the blood of Jesus, by a new and living way which He consecrated for us, through the veil, that is, His flesh, and having a High Priest over the house of God, let us draw near with a true heart in full assurance of faith, having our hearts sprinkled from an evil conscience and our bodies washed with pure water. (Hebrews 10:19–22)

BEYOND THE VEIL

Are you still unsure how to enter the Holiest? It is through the blood of Jesus. The boldness with which you are able to break through every barrier and enter the Holiest is not a conscious feeling of confidence; rather, it is the God-given right and liberty of entrance that Christ's blood assures you.

> To enter and live in the Holiest, you must believe that it is God's plan and purpose for you to dwell in this dimension.

When Christ entered into the heavenlies after His death on the cross and presented His blood to the Father on your behalf, God accepted it. That blood, and that blood alone, can bring you into the very presence and fellowship of the Father.

Boldness through Christ's blood has been secured. The living way into the Holiest has been prepared for you. Nothing remains to be accomplished. Will you enter in?

To enter and live in the Holiest, you must believe that it is God's plan and purpose for you to dwell in this powerful, supernatural dimension of His Spirit. Today, the tabernacle is gone, the temple is gone, and the ark of the covenant is gone. Now, *we* are the temple of the living God. His presence—in all His power and glory—is manifested in us. As you respond to the call of the Spirit, you are able to enter and live in the Holiest where there is a union and fellowship reserved for those who go beyond the veil. The supernatural power of God is released as a *result* of this intimate union with Christ where you are *one* with Him. The Father, Son, and Holy Spirit live, remain, commune, and release God's life in you.

Christians living in the Holiest have come to a place in their lives where they are totally dependent upon the presence of God for everything. They have died to self and recognize that without His presence and anointing, they are nothing and can do nothing. They live in such fellowship and union with Christ that they talk, act, and live according to the Spirit working in and through them. Again, Jesus said,

> *Abide in Me, and I in you. As the branch cannot bear fruit of itself, unless it abides in the vine, neither can you, unless you abide in Me. I am the vine, you are the branches. He who abides in Me, and I in him, bears much fruit; for without Me you can do nothing.* (John 15:4–5)

It is through this intimate union and relationship that you are able to walk in the supernatural and live in the fullness of Christ's power and glory. Not only has the way been opened for you to enter and live in the Holiest, but also, Christ, your Great High Priest, is there personally to receive you and give you access to all the blessings that the Father has for you. His work as Priest over the house of God is to bring you into the

Holiest and enable you to live there. *"We have such a High Priest, who is seated at the right hand of the throne of the Majesty in the heavens....And having a High Priest over the house of God, let us draw near with a true heart in full assurance of faith"* (Hebrews 8:1; 10:21–22).

The Father and Jesus, your Great High Priest, are waiting with outstretched arms. The Holy Spirit is calling you. What is your response to this call from the throne room of God to come and live in the Holiest, where the manifest presence of God resides?

The glory of God will rise upon the church. Greater than in the days when He manifested Himself in the midst of the children of Israel, He will manifest Himself in His church—to those who answer this call of the Spirit. *"Arise, shine; for your light has come! And the glory of the LORD is risen upon you"* (Isaiah 60:1).

Christians who are living in abiding, intimate relationship with God will experience the miraculous in their lives. If you haven't ventured beyond the veil and entered into the Holiest where you are living and breathing in God's manifest presence, pursue Him with all that is within you.

Don't be content where you are. Don't be satisfied with just enjoying His blessings in ministry or service. Your one abiding passion must be to run after Him. Abandon yourself to Him. Break through every barrier until His presence covers and enfolds you, and you are living in close, intimate fellowship with Him.

PERSONAL APPLICATION

Don't be content to remain in an "outer court" relationship with God. Pursue your heavenly Father with all that is within you!

1. Your personal time of prayer and communion with the Father must be the most important thing in your life. Refuse to allow yourself to become so caught up in day-to-day struggles and routines that you fail to commune with Him throughout the day. Arrange the rest of your schedule around the time you have set aside to be alone with Him. Refuse to allow anyone or anything to hinder you from this time of intimacy. Open your heart to the Father and share the things that concern you. Share your innermost desires, your frustrations, your goals, all the intimate longings of your heart.

2. David said, *"Seven times a day I praise You, because of Your righteous judgments"* (Psalm 119:164). Throughout the day, at home, at work, or wherever you go, praise Him for who He is and what He has done for you. Rekindle your first love for Him. Meditate on His blessings and the love He has showered upon you, and lavish your love upon Him.

CHAPTER ELEVEN

THESE SIGNS WILL FOLLOW

The task of the church is not to try to prove that miracles have not ceased and that God's power is just as real today as it was two thousand years ago. Instead, we need to humble ourselves before the Father and ask for the gifts of the Spirit to be stirred up within the body of Christ. For many years, we have depended upon the natural instead of looking to the supernatural power of God. It is time for us to yield ourselves into the hands of almighty God and earnestly pray for an outpouring of His Spirit that will shake us until we begin to operate in the fullness of His power. In this way, God's miracles will once again flow through us to demonstrate His love to a needy world and usher in the return of Jesus Christ.

There is no way we will be able to convince this world that Jesus came to earth, destroyed the works of the devil, died on the cross for our sins, rose from the dead, and has the power to save, heal, and deliver today, without a manifestation of His miracle-working power in our midst.

If we believe Christ's promise that we will do the same works as He did, we must act in faith and begin to *do* the same works.

Instead of being afraid to boldly proclaim God's miracle power for fear of what the world may think or because of the criticism or ridicule you may face from people in the church, you must have a fresh revelation of the power Christ intends you to have in fulfilling His purposes in these last days. Allow the words Jesus spoke as His final commission to the church to resonate in your spirit. These words are alive—they are pregnant with the life of God:

> *And these signs will follow those who believe: In My name they will cast out demons; they will speak with new tongues; they will take up serpents; and if they drink anything deadly, it will by no means hurt them; they will lay hands on the sick, and they will recover.* (Mark 16:17–18)

It is my prayer that these words will so burn within you that you will begin to move forward in the power of the Spirit to be all that Christ intended you to be.

PREACHING AND THE WORKING OF MIRACLES GO TOGETHER

In the church, we have often treated preaching and the working of miracles as separate aspects of ministry. There are very few churches where the Word is being preached with miracles accompanying it. While miracles are not to receive preeminence above the Word being preached, they are to complement it. We are not supposed to be seeking after miracles, but miracles, signs, and wonders are to *follow* all who believe!

MIRACLES TESTIFY TO THE WORLD

As we have seen, miracles are *visible proof* that the Word of God is true. It is not just any miracles, but miracles accompanying the true gospel of Jesus Christ, that testify to the truth. In Matthew 24:24, Christ warned us about false christs who would come on the scene and try to deceive people through their miracles. Yet Christ's purpose for His church is that supernatural works will be manifested *in His name* throughout the nations of the world as a final, end-time witness to the gospel. They are to demonstrate that there is salvation, healing, and deliverance in Jesus' name, and that He is coming soon.

Let's review how miracles are a witness to the reality and nature of Jesus Christ and His church.

MIRACLES TESTIFIED TO JESUS' MINISTRY

The works Christ did during His ministry on earth were…

- manifestations of God's power that proved to the world He was sent by the Father.
- visible proof that the Father was in Him and that He was the Son of God.
- confirmation of the message that He preached.

When John the Baptist was imprisoned by Herod, he asked Jesus through his disciples if He was the promised Messiah, or if they should expect someone else. Jesus replied to John's disciples,

> *Go and tell John the things which you hear and see: the blind see and the lame walk; the lepers are cleansed and the deaf hear; the dead are raised up and the poor have the gospel preached to them.* (Matthew 11:4–5)

Jesus spoke about His works—about the miracles He had done. The miracles *testified* that He was who He claimed to be.

Another time, Jesus told the Jews who asked Him if He was the Christ,

> *The works that I do in My Father's name, they bear witness of Me....If I do not do the works of My Father, do not believe Me; but if I do, though you do not believe Me, believe the works, that you may know and believe that the Father is in Me, and I in Him.* (John 10:25, 37–38)

If they didn't believe what He said, they were to believe the works He did as proof that the Father was in Him, and He was in the Father.

Jesus did not claim to do these works by His own power. He told His disciples the works He did were accomplished by the Father within Him.

> *Do you not believe that I am in the Father, and the Father is in Me? The words that I say to you I do not speak on My own initiative, but the Father abiding in Me does His works. Believe Me that I am in the Father and the Father in Me; otherwise believe because of the works themselves.* (John 14:10–11 NASB)

The key to the flow of the miracle power of God through Jesus, which enabled Him to do the works of His Father, was the fact that the Father was living within Him. *"God anointed Jesus of Nazareth with the Holy Spirit and with power, who went about doing good and healing all who were oppressed by the devil, for God was with Him"* (Acts 10:38). God anointed Jesus with His Spirit and *dunamis* power. Jesus said,

> *If I bear witness of Myself, My witness is not true....But I have a greater witness than John's; for the works which the*

Father has given Me to finish; the very works that I do; bear witness of Me, that the Father has sent Me. (John 5:31, 36)

Jesus had a witness far greater than any human witness. The miracles and mighty demonstrations of God's power were His witnesses. The miracles manifested through Jesus were the *result* of the life of almighty God flowing through Him. They were a reflection of that truth.

> **The miracles manifested through Jesus were the *result* of the life of almighty God flowing through Him.**

The reason Jesus said miracles will follow us as the church, and that we will be able to do even greater works than He did, is found in John 14:12: *"Most assuredly, I say to you, he who believes in Me, the works that I do he will do also; and greater works than these he will do, **because I go to My Father**"* (emphasis added). In this statement, He gave the disciples a glimpse into the future outpouring of the Holy Spirit upon them.

> *And I will pray the Father, and He will give you another Helper, that He may abide with you forever; the Spirit of truth, whom the world cannot receive, because it neither sees Him nor knows Him; but you know Him, for He dwells with you and will be in you....But the Helper, the Holy Spirit, whom the Father will send in My name, He will teach you all things, and bring to your remembrance all things that I said to you.* (John 14:16–17, 26)

This was a moment of great spiritual destiny. Jesus knew that the disciples needed more than what they currently possessed in order to live for God. In His final moments with them, He wanted to impart something into their lives that would sustain them in the days to follow. He was preparing them for the time He would no longer be with them. He told them that *because He was going to the Father,* all those who believed in Him would do the same works He had done, and greater.

He promised that He was going to send the Helper to them and that they would be witnesses of Him as a result.

> *But you shall receive power when the Holy Spirit has come upon you; and you shall be witnesses to Me in Jerusalem, and in all Judea and Samaria, and to the end of the earth.*
>
> (Acts 1:8)

When Jesus said, *"You shall be witnesses,"* He was not only referring to a verbal witness and proclamation of the gospel. He was referring to the manifestation of the power of the Holy Spirit that would flow through all those who were baptized, saturated, and controlled by the Holy Spirit.

MIRACLES TESTIFIED TO THE EARLY CHURCH'S MINISTRY

The miracles of healing and deliverance manifested in the lives of the disciples testified of the reality of the gospel they preached. During His ministry, Jesus called His twelve disciples together, commissioned them, and sent them forth with *signs* and *wonders* as their credentials.

> *And when He had called His twelve disciples to Him, He gave them power over unclean spirits, to cast them out, and to heal all kinds of sickness and all kinds of disease....*[Jesus commanded them,] *"And as you go, preach, saying, 'The*

*kingdom of heaven is at hand.' Heal the sick, cleanse the
lepers, raise the dead, cast out demons. Freely you have received, freely give."* (Matthew 10:1, 7–8)

The disciples had been with Jesus for some time hearing
His doctrine concerning the kingdom, learning how to pray,
and witnessing the signs and wonders He performed. Now,
the time had come for them to go into the villages and towns
proclaiming the kingdom of God.

The commission was twofold:

1. To preach the kingdom of heaven and call the people to
   repentance
2. To minister to the desperate needs of the people through
   the manifestation of miracles done in His name

Jesus did not hesitate for a moment when He told His disciples they would do the same works and even greater works
than He had done. He knew He was sending the Holy Spirit to
live within them, and that the same power at work within Him
would manifest miracles through them. The Holy Spirit would
give them spiritual gifts that would equip them to meet the
needs of the body of Christ and to reach a lost world.

Jesus set the pattern for the church to follow. We are to
preach and proclaim the Word with miracles and signs following. Jesus said that believers would have the same power and
authority to do the works He had done...

- To heal the sick
- To cast out demons
- To raise the dead
- To have authority over nature

WALKING IN THE SUPERNATURAL

The miracles that were manifested in the early church bore *witness* of the disciples. They were living proof that Christ was *in them* and that the same Holy Spirit that flowed through Christ was flowing through them.

> *And* [Jesus] *said to them, "Go into all the world and preach the gospel to every creature. He who believes and is baptized will be saved; but he who does not believe will be condemned. And these* **signs** *will follow those who believe....And they went out and preached everywhere, the Lord working with them and confirming the word through the accompanying signs.* (Mark 16:15–17, 20, emphasis added)

> *Then He called His twelve disciples together and gave them power and authority over all demons, and to cure diseases. He sent them to preach the kingdom of God and to heal the sick.* (Luke 9:1–2)

> *So great a salvation, which at the first began to be spoken by the Lord, and was* **confirmed to us by those who heard Him**, **God also bearing witness both with signs and wonders**, *with various miracles, and gifts of the Holy Spirit, according to His own will.*
> (Hebrews 2:3–4, emphasis added)

Jesus did not separate preaching from the working of miracles. He considered them both an integral part of the commission He had given the disciples. Moreover, this commission did not apply only to the twelve apostles. After Jesus had sent them out, He appointed seventy other disciples, commissioned them, and gave them miracles as their credentials.

> *After these things the Lord appointed seventy others also, and sent them two by two before His face into every city and*

place where He Himself was about to go. Then He said to them, "...heal the sick there, and say to them, 'The kingdom of God has come near to you.'" (Luke 10:1–2, 9)

The disciples had depended upon Jesus and the authority and power He had delegated to them while He was with them to minister healing and deliverance. As long as He was with them, they had His authority and power, but these things were not permanently residing in them until they were baptized in the Holy Spirit.

> Jesus equipped the church with His miracle power so we would be able to set people free from the bondage of Satan.

When Jesus returned to the Father, He sent the Holy Spirit to live and remain in them. With the coming of the Holy Spirit, the authority and power to work miracles in His name *remained* in Jesus' followers. Although Christ no longer was with them in His physical body, they did mighty works through the Holy Spirit and in the authority of Jesus' name.

MIRACLES TESTIFY TO OUR MINISTRY TODAY

For hundreds of years, the church has been busy proclaiming the Word of God, but it has largely failed to manifest the accompanying miracles to meet the desperate needs of humanity.

Jesus empowered and equipped the church with His miracle power so we would be able to set people free from the bondage of Satan and loose them from their infirmities. He infused the church with the power of the Holy Spirit, so that we would be able to carry on the *same ministry* He had upon the earth.

- Miracles *bear witness* that Christ is living within us.
- Miracles *confirm* the gospel we preach.

In the ministry of Maria Woodworth-Etter, who lived in the 1800s, God's miracle power was manifested in a powerful way and was used to help bring revival to various parts of America. As people saw and experienced the supernatural power of God for themselves, they turned to Christ by the thousands. The following is just one exciting account from Maria Woodworth-Etter of the move of God in St. Louis, Missouri, in 1890:

> A little girl was brought to me one day; she was altogether helpless, could not talk or walk and had no use of herself. I prayed for her. The crowd was great as there were hundreds trying to step into the pool, so we told them to take her out a little and let her try to walk, for she might walk at once, or they might have to teach her, like any other child learning to walk. After a while, they came back with her. She was walking and talking, but they could not understand a word she said! Praise the Lord, she had the use of her whole body; she was walking and talking in a strange language or tongue. She was filled with the Spirit and as bold as a lion in the power of the Holy Spirit.
>
> I stood her on the platform, and she began to walk about and preach. With hands uplifted, pointing to heaven, and stamping her foot, she preached to the

astonished multitude, showing what great things the Lord had done for her, for she spoke some words in English.

...The whole city was shaken. Missions started in many places. The different churches began to have street meetings and to visit the prisons and hospitals as they had never done before.[30]

Mrs. Woodworth-Etter said of her meetings, "The mouths of the gainsayers, scoffers, and liars were stopped. Thousands of souls were saved."[31]

Through the *same* anointing of the Holy Spirit, which was released upon the disciples in the early church and has been released in the lives of various Christians for two thousand years, Christ has planned for every born-again believer to walk in the supernatural—manifesting the *same* miracle-working power that was manifested in His life.

Over a period of years of praying and believing God for miracles and deliverances, I have been privileged to see unusual and mighty wonders, and I have often been asked, "What is the greatest miracle of healing you have witnessed?" Let this account of what happened in an evangelistic crusade in India build your faith to receive what you need from God and to reach out in ministry to others.

One evening, as I was ministering, the Holy Spirit moved across the great audience with a visible manifestation of His glory. A cloud of His presence appeared over the congregation, seen by all. Suddenly, a leper, who had been standing at the back of the crowd, ran around the edge of the gathering and leaped up onto the platform. He grabbed the microphone from my hand and began shouting at the top of his voice. Over and over, he kept repeating the same phrase. I asked the interpreter what was happening, and he told me the man was shouting, "I'm healed! I'm healed! I'm healed!"

We asked the leper to tell his story.

He lived in a leper colony nearly a hundred miles away from where we were having the meeting. He had heard about the crusade and requested permission to leave the hospital and come for prayer. He felt that if he could just get to the crusade, he would receive his healing. Since his leprosy was in an advanced stage, however, the administrators were fearful about his leaving, and they withheld permission.

> **The leprosy disappeared from the man's body like frost disappears from a windshield!**

He ignored their advice, slipped quietly away, and headed toward the meeting. The leper walked much of the one hundred miles, sneaking rides in the backs of vehicles part of the way. When he reached the location where our crusade was being held, the service was beginning. As he stood at the back of the crowd of some forty thousand people, he suddenly felt something strange and looked down at his hands. The way he described what happened was amazing—it was like when you turn on the defroster in a car and watch it defrost the windshield.

"I saw the leprosy departing," he shouted, "beginning at the ends of my fingers and moving up my hands and arms." His hands and the rest of his body were completely clear of the leprous sores!

The crowd went wild as the man leaped, danced, and shouted for joy. They were so moved by his testimony that hundreds rushed forward to accept Christ as their Savior.

At the close of the service some time later, a gentleman approached me. He owned one of the largest newspapers in southern India. He had seen how the man with leprosy had been healed, and he said, "You are to come to my home tomorrow morning at seven and pray for my son, who is an invalid. He is seven years old and has never walked a step in his life."

He continued, "If your God heals my son, I will become a Christian and use all of my resources to help propagate the gospel of Jesus Christ throughout all of India."

I said, "Sir, I'll be happy to come and minister to your son. You cannot buy God's blessings. If he is healed, it will be through the power of the Lord Jesus Christ, God's only Son, the only Savior."

Early the next morning, his driver arrived where I was staying and drove me to his house. I thought that I would just go and pray for the boy and then come back to my room. I was surprised to see the yard, porch, courtyard, and inside of the house filled with people. I recognized it as an opportunity to present the gospel to people who might not otherwise hear it, and I began talking with them. The Scripture says that faith comes by hearing and hearing by the Word of God.

As I spoke, I discerned a rising level of faith in the people. Looking across the room, my eyes caught the eyes of a woman seated there, and the Holy Spirit told me she was suffering intense pain and a high fever. I told her what God had revealed to me and she screamed, "How did you know that? I have told no one!" I explained that the Spirit had revealed it to me and that God would heal her if she would accept it.

As I prayed for her, a wonderful transformation of peace came upon her. She started rejoicing and shouting, "I'm healed! The pain is gone! The fever is gone!" The faith of the people soared even higher when they heard her testimony.

I said to the man with the crippled boy, "Now is the time to pray for your son."

He brought the boy to me and placed him in my arms. The little boy was perhaps the most handsome child I had ever seen, but his little legs were like rubber. He had absolutely no control of them.

I prayed for him and immediately sensed a confirmation that God was healing him. I started to hand him back to his father and announced that God had begun the healing. I instructed the father that since his boy had never walked, he would need to teach him to take his first steps, just as babies must be taught to walk.

The father surprised me with his response. "No, if your God has really healed my son, he is able to walk now!"

At that moment, I thought of the two accounts of healings of crippled people in the New Testament, the man at the Gate Beautiful in Acts 3 and the man at the Pool of Bethesda in John 5. Both of them had been lame all their lives and no one had to teach them how to take first steps. One of them leaped and danced immediately; the other took up his bed and walked, not having walked for at least thirty-eight years.

THESE SIGNS WILL FOLLOW

I looked around at the waiting crowd and then back at the hopeful father. I prayed a short prayer, saying, "Lord, if You did it for that man at the temple and that man at Bethesda, You can do it for this seven-year-old child!"

I walked across the room and, as I put the boy down on the floor, I said, "Son, when I release you, I want you to walk across the room to where your father is standing." To the amazement and joy of everyone watching, he not only walked, but he also ran and jumped into his father's arms!

The father went back to his newspaper that day and printed a special edition of his paper. The headline read, "T. L. Lowery from the U.S. healing people of leprosy, deafness and all manner of afflictions."

> To the amazement and joy of everyone watching, the boy not only walked, but he also ran and jumped into his father's arms!

Are you ready to move into this supernatural dimension in which God's miracle power is flowing through you?

Are you expecting God to work miracles through you?

Are signs and wonders following you?

Pastors and ministers of the gospel, are you preaching the Word with miracles accompanying and confirming the Word? Whom are you listening to? What are you going to believe—the teaching of man-made doctrines or the Word of God?

Through the years, God has raised up and anointed men and women like Smith Wigglesworth, John G. Lake, Maria

Woodworth-Etter, Kathryn Kuhlman, T. L. Osborne, Oral Roberts, Morris Cerullo, Benny Hinn, and Reinhard Bonnke, just to name a few. God has called out and chosen men and women like these and many others, and He has used them mightily in manifesting His supernatural power. However, remember that He did not intend for only a few select individuals to manifest this power, which has generally been the case for hundreds of years. Christ planned for His body on earth to be infused with His authority and power to work miracles in His name.

Jesus did not limit the working of signs and miracles to His disciples or those who had already developed great faith. As He prepared to go to the cross, He said, *"He who believes in Me, the works that I do he will do also; and greater works than these he will do, because I go to My Father"* (John 14:12). Notice that Jesus didn't say "maybe" or "perhaps" believers would do even greater works. He left no doubt whatsoever concerning what He meant. He said *those who believe in Him* will not only do the same works but even *greater* works. We have read these Scriptures and heard them taught for years, but where is the reality and fulfillment of them within the lives of most Christians today?

The church is to be a *full manifestation* of all that Christ is to meet the critical needs in the world and fulfill His end-time purposes. Recall that Jesus wasn't depending upon any natural abilities the disciples and other early believers possessed that would enable them to do the same miraculous works He had done. And He is not depending upon any natural abilities or talents you possess. He said, *"These signs will follow those who **believe***" (Mark 16:17, emphasis added).

THESE SIGNS WILL FOLLOW

POWER AND AUTHORITY IN HIS NAME

As the seventy followers of Jesus whom He commissioned went into the towns and villages, they went in His name and in power. Signs followed them! As they preached, they cast out demons and healed the sick. When they returned to Jesus, they were filled with excitement, saying, *"Lord, even the demons are subject to us in Your name"* (Luke 10:17). Jesus answered them,

> *I saw Satan falling like a lightning [flash] from heaven. Behold! I have given you authority and power to trample upon serpents and scorpions, and [physical and mental strength and ability] over all the power that the enemy [possesses]; and nothing shall in any way harm you.*
>
> (Luke 10:18–19 AMP)

Jesus gave them authority and power *in His name* over all the power of the enemy, so they would be fully equipped to fulfill the work He had given them to do. Likewise, He was not just giving us a formula for prayer when He told us to pray in His name. (See John 14:13–14; 15:16; 16:23–27.) He has commissioned and sent us forth in His authority and power. As we face the attacks of the enemy—sin, sickness, disease, demon possession, and even death—in the power and authority of Jesus' name, the words we speak in His name will be fulfilled.

During His final hours with His disciples before He went to the cross, Jesus repeatedly emphasized the authority and power He had given them through His name. He told them, *"You did not choose Me, but I chose you and appointed you that you should go and bear fruit, and that your fruit should remain, that* whatever you ask the Father **in My name** He may give you" (John 15:16 NASB, emphasis added).

As He spoke to them that night, Jesus knew He was soon going out into battle to face Satan.

He knew He would be scourged, mocked, and beaten.

He knew He would be walking the lonely road to Calvary.

He knew He would hang on the cross—taking all our sins upon Himself—and die.

> **To walk in the supernatural, you must begin to exercise and release the authority and power Christ has given you.**

He knew the disciples would be discouraged and filled with sorrow because of His death and because He would no longer be with them.

Yet He also knew that in a little while—in three short days—He would rise in triumph, and that in a little more than a month He would ascend to the Father, where He would be seated in a position of supreme power and authority over all things. Through the outpouring of the Holy Spirit, He would invest in them this same authority and power and, as they went forth in His name, the words they spoke—whatever they asked—would come to pass.

Look again at what Jesus told the disciples during their final meeting before the cross:

> *I assure you, most solemnly I tell you, if any one steadfastly believes in Me, he will himself be able to do the things that*

I do; and he will do even greater things than these, because I go to the Father. And I will do [I Myself will grant] whatever you ask in My Name [as presenting all that I AM], so that the Father may be glorified and extolled in (through) the Son. [Yes] I will grant [I Myself will do for you] whatever you shall ask in My Name [as presenting all that I AM]. (John 14:12–14 AMP)

TAKE HOLD OF THE LEGAL AUTHORITY AND POWER THAT BELONGS TO YOU

Think about the legal authority and power you have been given in Jesus' name.

- Jesus' name is all-powerful, indestructible, and unchangeable.
- All the fullness of the Godhead is in His name.
- There is salvation in His name.
- There is healing in His name.
- There is creative power in His name.
- There is deliverance in His name.
- Everything we need is in His name!

Think also about the tremendous price Jesus paid to give us the authority and power of His name. To walk in the supernatural with miracles and signs following, as Jesus promised, you must begin to exercise and release the authority and power Christ has given you. The basis for your doing the same works as Jesus is the same as it was for the early church:

1. Jesus has defeated Satan and all the powers of darkness. He has given you authority over them in His name.

2. Jesus has sent the Holy Spirit to live and dwell within you, giving you the same *dunamis* power that flowed through Him.

3. Jesus has invested within you all the power that is in His name—the name that is above every other name.

In the Spirit, reach out and take hold of the authority and power He has given you. It legally belongs to you, but unless you reach out by faith, take it, and use it in your circumstances, it will never be realized in your life. Don't listen to Satan's lies that you are just an insignificant person, and that you cannot do the same miraculous works Jesus did. Don't cast aside the authority and power Jesus has given you in His name.

ENTER THE PROMISED LAND

In Hebrews 4:2, we read about an entire generation of the children of Israel who saw God's mighty works but failed to enter the land He had promised. They heard God's promises, but they did not take possession of the land because *"the word which they heard did not profit them, not being mixed with faith in those who heard it."*

As God's people today, we must not fail, through our lack of faith, to move into the fulfillment of Christ's promises that His power will flow through us. Regardless of what you may have been taught or how you feel, it *is* possible for you to walk in the supernatural. In this end-time hour, God is releasing the wind of the Holy Spirit to breathe upon His church. He is raising up a remnant of people who are living in covenant with Him, who are in tune with the Holy Spirit, and who are stepping out in answer to His call to fulfill His will on earth through an awesome manifestation of His supernatural power. As they are yielded to and controlled by the Holy Spirit, the *dunamis* power will be released through them. We haven't seen anything yet!

Miracles are your credentials, proving that you are a son or daughter of a mighty, supernatural God. We must not seek power, but rather seek to be saturated, controlled, and directed by the Holy Spirit. The Holy Spirit working in us will produce the results. Instead of making excuses for why God's miracle power isn't being manifested much today, we need to repent of our unbelief and cry out to God for a fresh release of His mighty power.

> **Seek to be saturated with, yielded to, and directed by the Holy Spirit.**

Remember that, after Peter and John were commanded not to preach or teach in the name of Jesus and were then released, they returned to the believers and called the church together to pray. They did not trust in their own abilities. They cried out to God to stretch forth His hand to work miracles in their midst in the name of Jesus. (See Acts 4:29–30.) God answered their prayer with a supernatural manifestation of His power. He shook the place where they were gathered together, and they were all filled with the Holy Spirit and began to speak the Word with boldness. They went everywhere preaching the Word and working miracles in the name of Jesus.

It is going to take the same type of manifestation of God's power within and among us today to get the job done of reaching the world with the gospel. We need the Spirit of the living God to be poured out upon us until we are shaken by His power and are so full of the Holy Spirit that we begin to walk in His power. It is time for every born-again, Holy Spirit-baptized believer to face the sicknesses, family situations, financial problems, and other adverse circumstances that come into their lives and those around them, with the supernatural, miracle-working power of God.

God doesn't want you to see Him just as the God who performed miracles thousands of years ago for Israel and the early church. He wants you to see Him as the God of miracles *today* and to expect Him to supernaturally manifest Himself through miracles on your behalf *today*. To walk in the supernatural, with the miracle-working power of God manifested in your life, begin to take the following vital steps.

1. KNOW THAT YOU HAVE THE POWER TO DO THE SAME WORKS JESUS DID

Miracles are the result of Christ living within you and the flow of the Holy Spirit working through you. As you are fully yielded to and led by the Holy Spirit, the *dunamis,* miracle power of God will flow out of you to do His works. You must not just hear this but *know* this for it to be a reality in your life.

2. BEGIN TO MINISTER TO THE DESPERATE NEEDS AROUND YOU IN A DEMONSTRATION OF POWER

Begin right where you are to minister to the needs of those within your family, your neighborhood, your church, and on the job. The miracle power of God was released through the disciples in the early church as they began to preach the gospel everywhere they went. As you minister to the needs of others according to the direction of the Holy Spirit, the power of God will be released through you to meet whatever need is present.

3. BELIEVE AND EXPECT GOD'S MIRACLE POWER TO BE RELEASED THROUGH YOU.

In whatever ministry God directs you to do, expect His power to be released. Don't limit what God will do through you. Don't depend upon natural human ability to meet the need. Knowing it is His will to manifest His power through you, expect Him to meet the need supernaturally.

Are you looking beyond the natural into the supernatural and believing God for His provision for your life? Are you allowing God to use you to manifest miracles to meet the desperate needs of those around you? I urge you to receive this revelation deep into your spirit.

BAPTIZED WITH POWER

If you have not yet been baptized in the Holy Spirit, earnestly begin to seek the Lord, asking Him to baptize you and fill you to overflowing with His Spirit. *"He will baptize you with the Holy Spirit and fire"* (Matthew 3:11). To be baptized in the Spirit does not just mean to be full or even full to overflowing with the Spirit. It means to be totally *immersed*—totally saturated—with the Holy Spirit. It is through this baptism of power that you will be able to walk in the supernatural and do the same works that Jesus did.

Let me relate what happened when I was in Gastonia, North Carolina, conducting a crusade in the city auditorium. In a special healing service, I preached a faith message and then people formed a prayer line around that large auditorium. I began to pray and minister to those who had come forward.

The first lady in line was a Baptist. She said, "Brother Lowery, I have not come for healing; I have come to receive the Holy Spirit."

I said, "Sister, lift your hands in faith and believe God. When I lay hands upon you, expect God to impart to you the gift of the Holy Spirit."

She lifted her hands, and when I laid my hands upon her, a heavy anointing came on her and she fell prostrate under the power of God. Suddenly she began to speak with other tongues as the Spirit flowed freely and beautifully through her.

> **Are you allowing God to use you to manifest miracles to meet the desperate needs of those around you?**

Behind her in the line was a Presbyterian lady. She said, "Brother Lowery, I came to be healed, but I would rather have what that Baptist lady received than be healed!"

I said, "All right, raise your hands." I laid my hands on her, and the same marvelous thing happened. She fell prostrate under the power right beside the Baptist lady and began to speak in other tongues as the Spirit gave her the ability.

That is something of a miracle in itself. If you can get a Baptist and a Presbyterian to lie down beside one another, you are doing something!

Behind her was a Methodist lady. She said, "Oh, I came for the Holy Spirit!"

I said, "All right, raise your hands, and when I lay hands on you expect a miracle."

Before I could pray for her, the chairman of the meeting told me that she was a Methodist minister's wife. "She shouldn't ask for the Holy Spirit if she doesn't want Him," I said, and laid hands on her. The same wonderful thing happened to her that had happened to the other ladies—she received the baptism in the Holy Spirit and began to speak in other tongues through the power of the Spirit.

Jesus is the Baptizer. As John the Baptist said, *"He will baptize you with the Holy Spirit and fire"* (Matthew 3:11, emphasis added). Jesus told His disciples,

> *Behold, I send the Promise of my Father upon you.*
> (Luke 24:49)

> *If I depart, I will send Him to you.*   (John 16:7)

The baptism in the Holy Spirit is a personal encounter with the Holy Spirit, the third person of the Trinity, which produces a continual flow of God's power in your life. Jesus is the Source of this life-giving stream of the Holy Spirit. Many Christians are seeking power or other manifestations of the Spirit instead of seeking the Source—the Baptizer of the Holy Spirit. To walk in the supernatural, you must come to Jesus.

> *[Jesus said,] "If anyone thirsts, let him come to Me and drink. He who believes in Me, as the Scripture has said,*

out of his heart will flow rivers of living water." But this He spoke concerning the Spirit, whom those believing in Him would receive; for the Holy Spirit was not yet given, because Jesus was not yet glorified. (John 7:37–39)

Jesus was not talking about giving them a drink of physical water, and He was not referring to the new life we receive when we are born again. He was talking about the outpouring of the Holy Spirit into our lives, and He said the *"living water"* would be *overflowing*. He didn't say there would be a trickle of water. He said that out of our innermost being would flow *"rivers of living water"*—rivers of the Holy Spirit to meet the needs of those around us.

Without a continual intake of the life-giving Spirit, you will spiritually dry up. You must keep coming and drinking so that you are totally immersed—totally possessed and controlled by the Holy Spirit. Come and receive a fresh intake of the Spirit. Be continually filled to overflowing with the Holy Spirit, and you will walk in His power and anointing.

The Spirit of God is bringing you now to a point in your life where you must make a commitment to be willing to do whatever is necessary to come into a greater relationship with Christ, where the same power and anointing He had is in you. To walk in the supernatural, an unquenchable thirst and longing for God to totally possess your being must be the continual desire of your heart.

WALK IN SUPERNATURAL POWER

In this book, I have opened my heart and shared the revelation God has given me. I have personally witnessed the awesome, miraculous power of God, and His miracle power has flowed through me. Blind eyes have been opened. Deaf ears have been unstopped. Lepers have been cleansed, helpless crippled have walked—all types of sicknesses have been healed. Beyond any doubt, I know it is God's will for His sons and daughters to walk in the supernatural today, with a daily expectation of the manifestation of His miracle power in their lives.

The church must raise its voice in unity worldwide and pray, "Lord, do it again! Pour out Your Spirit! Release Your power through us to bring healing and deliverance to the nations in Jesus' name. Make known and magnify Your great name and power in this generation. Give us holy boldness to preach Your Word without fear and compromise. Stretch out Your hand to heal and manifest signs and wonders as a witness to the world that You are the one true and living God."

> **The church must pray in unity worldwide, "Lord, pour out Your Spirit! Release Your power through us to bring healing and deliverance to the nations in Jesus' name."**

I have shared with you how to break through your own personal environment and begin to walk in daily anticipation that God's supernatural power will be released within you. Don't let this be just another inspiring message that you read, put on the bookshelf, and then forget. Spend time in prayer asking God to manifest these truths in your life. Then, act on what God reveals to you.

WALKING IN THE SUPERNATURAL

You have been created anew in the image of Christ and filled with the supernatural power of God to do the same mighty works He did. Begin to live and walk every day of your life in the supernatural power of almighty God!

THESE SIGNS WILL FOLLOW

PERSONAL APPLICATION

Miracles are your credentials. They are part of your spiritual DNA as a son or daughter of almighty God. To walk in the supernatural...

1. Focus on the promises Christ has given you:

> *You did not choose Me, but I chose you and appointed you that you should go and bear fruit, and that your fruit should remain, that whatever you ask the Father in My name He may give you.* (John 15:16)

> *He who believes in Me, the works that I do he will do also; and greater works than these he will do, because I go to My Father.* (John 14:12)

> *These signs will follow those who believe: In My name they will cast out demons; they will speak with new tongues; ...they will lay hands on the sick, and they will recover.* (Mark 16:17–18)

2. Make the following a daily confession of your faith:

> I am born-again, baptized by the power of the Holy Spirit. I am a supernatural being, filled with the supernatural power of God, created in the image of Christ. Through His Spirit within me, I have the same miracle-working power as Christ had, to do the same mighty works He did. Today, I am believing and expecting His miracle power to be released within me to meet the desperate needs of those around me.

3. Ask the Lord to direct you daily to someone in need. Jesus said, *"Freely you have received, freely give"* (Matthew 10:8). Just as Peter reached down to the lame man and said, *"What I do have I give you: In the name of Jesus Christ of Nazareth, rise up and walk"* (Acts 3:6), minister to those the Holy Spirit directs you to in Jesus' name, knowing that His miracle-working power will be released through you.

4. Whatever God has placed upon your heart to do, whether it is an inner-city outreach, a home Bible study, a prison outreach, a hospital or nursing-home ministry, or anything else—minister to the needs of the people in a demonstration of God's power. Remove all limits you may have placed upon God to work miracles through you. Remember that God is not depending upon anything you possess in the natural. Yield yourself fully to the Holy Spirit and release your faith, believing that God's miracle power will be released.

NOTES

Chapter 1, Spiritual Megathrust

[1] <http://en.wikipedia.org/wiki/2004_Indian_Ocean_earthquake> (November 17, 2006)

[2] <http://www.joshuaproject.net/globalstatistics.php> (December 21, 2006)

[3] Paul and Joy Hattaway, *Asia Harvest* newsletter #67, July 2002, 2. <http://www.asiaharvest.org/pages/newsletters/67%20-%20July%20 2002%20-%20Henan%20Province%20(Part%203).pdf> (December 13, 2006)

[4] Ibid, 9.

[5] Dennis and Joy Balcombe, *The Challenge of China: Ministry Report of RCMI* (Revival Chinese Ministries International), Summer 2001. <http://www.rcmi.ac/eng/html/newsletter/summer01/e_rose.htm> (December 13, 2006)

[6] The Friday Fax: News from India and Worldwide (2005, #32), www.bufton.net/fridayfax. <http://www.jesus.org.uk/dawn/2005/ dawn32.html> (December 13, 2006)

[7] Dennis and Joy Balcombe, *The Challenge of China: Ministry Report of RCMI* (Revival Chinese Ministries International), January 1997. <http://www.rcmi.ac/eng/html/newsletter/jan97/e_testimonies. htm>(December 15, 2006)

Chapter 2, A New Paradigm

[8] Dr. Bill Hamon, *The Day of the Saints* (Shippensburg, PA: Destiny Image, 2002), 15, 19 (Introduction).

[9] Ibid., 31.

[10] George Barna, *Revolution* (Carol Stream, IL: Barna Books [an imprint of Tyndale House Publishers], 2005), 9.

[11] Ibid., 13–14.

[12] Ibid., 15.

[13] Ibid., 17.

[14] Ibid., 38.

[15] Ibid., 33, 32, 31.

Chapter 6, Developing Supernatural Eyesight

[16] Peter Madden, *The Wigglesworth Standard* (New Kensington, PA: Whitaker House, 1993), 146.

[17] Ibid., 97–98.

[18] Smith Wigglesworth, *Ever Increasing Faith* (New Kensington, PA: Whitaker House, 2000), 176–177.

[19] Albert Hibbert, *Smith Wigglesworth: The Secret of His Power* (Tulsa, OK: Harrison House, 1982, 1993), 42–44.

[20] Andrew Murray, *With Christ in the School of Prayer* (New Kensington, PA: Whitaker House, (1981), 81.

Chapter 7, Your Vital Link to the Supernatural

[21] Ronald F. Youngblood, gen. ed., *Nelson's New Illustrated Bible Dictionary* (Nashville: Thomas Nelson Publishers, 1995, 1986), "Hope," 575 (author's emphasis).

[22] Brother Yun and Paul Hattaway, *The Heavenly Man* (Grand Rapids, MI: Monarch Press, 2002), 299–300.

Chapter 8, Possessing God's DNA

[23] Lance Wubbels, comp. and ed., *Andrew Murray on Holiness: A 30-Day Devotional Treasury* (Lynwood, WA: Emerald Books, 2002), Day 10.

Chapter 9, God's Manifest Presence

[24] Charles Finney, *Holy Spirit Revivals* (New Kensington, PA: Whitaker House, 1999), 81.

[25] Frank Bartleman, *Azusa Street* (New Kensington, PA: Whitaker House, 1982), 72.

[26] Renny McLean, *Eternity Invading Time* (Longwood, Florida: Advantage Books, 2005), 25.

[27] George Barna, *Revolution* (Carol Stream, IL: Barna Books [an imprint of Tyndale House Publishers], 2005, 31–32.

NOTES

Chapter 10, Living in the Holiest

[28] A. W. Tozer, *The Pursuit of God* (Camp Hill, PA: Christian Publications, 1982, 1993), 36.

[29] See Merrill F. Unger and R. K. Harrison, ed., *The New Unger's Bible Dictionary* (Chicago: Moody Press, 1988), 1238.

Chapter 11, These Signs Will Follow

[30] Maria Woodworth-Etter, *Signs and Wonders* (New Kensington, PA: Whitaker House, 1997), 105–106.

[31] Ibid., 107.

ABOUT THE AUTHOR

The ministry of T. L. Lowery during a sixty-year career has been marked by three divine assignments: he has served as an evangelist, a pastor, and a denominational executive. In each season of ministry, his work has been anointed by the Holy Spirit and blessed with success.

As an evangelist, Dr. T. L. Lowery has placed the proclamation of the Word in power for spiritual transformation as the central theme of his ministry. In whatever office he has held, he has been a soulwinner. For fifteen years he crisscrossed the nation with a tent that held 10,000 worshippers, impacting cities and regions with the power of the gospel. He preached in scores of conventions, camp meetings, and citywide gatherings with a legacy of thousands of converts, people healed, and believers filled with the Spirit. His evangelistic ministry has taken him to 115 nations of the world.

He has been a pastor of two great churches: North Cleveland Church of God, the flagship church of its denomination and one of the oldest continually existing Pentecostal churches in the world, and the National Church of God, a growing church that serves the nation's capital. In the twenty years he led these two churches, membership in each increased exponentially, successive building programs gave the congregations great sanctuaries and educational plants, homes for retired persons were constructed, and hundreds of members were discipled and sent out for ministry. The churches became drawing boards and models for the training of other pastors.

As a denominational executive, Dr. Lowery has brought dimensions of faith and vision to his leadership posts. Serving sixteen years on the Executive Committee, the five-man group of top leaders of the Church of God, and thirty-four years on the Executive Council, its highest elected governing body, he has furnished visionary leadership and caring ministry to pastors.

Presently, Dr. Lowery serves as an exemplary model for today's evangelists, pastors, and church leaders. Through the T. L. Lowery Global Foundation, he shares biblical teaching about apostolic ministry and introduces these principles to a new generation of young men and women of God. The goal is to encourage effective ministry through his example of faithful servanthood.

In addition to an earned Ph.D. degree, Dr. Lowery has been recognized by two institutions with honorary doctorates. He is the author or coauthor of two dozen books, many of which have been translated into numerous languages.

During his years of ministry, his wife, Mildred Woodard Lowery, has labored faithfully alongside him and has graced his ministry with her compassionate nature and discerning spirit. Their son, Stephen Lowery, who followed his father as pastor of the National Church of God congregation, ministers in the same anointing.